Personal Truths

Youth Utilizing Artmaking to Promote Diversity, Equity, Inclusion, and Belonging

A Volume in
Promoting Justice, Diversity, and Inclusivity
Through Arts-Based Practices

Series Editor

Christa Boske
Kent State University

Promoting Justice, Diversity, and Inclusivity Through Arts-Based Practices

Christa Boske, Series Editor

Personal Truths: Youth Utilizing Artmaking to Promote Diversity, Equity, Inclusion, and Belonging (2025)
by Christa Boske

Children With Learning Differences Exploring Artmaking to Address Deficit-Laden Perspectives (2023)
edited by Christa Boske

The Time is Now: Creating Community Through Social Justice Artmaking (2022)
edited by Christa Boske

Personal Truths

Youth Utilizing Artmaking to Promote Diversity, Equity, Inclusion, and Belonging

by

Christa Boske
Kent State University

INFORMATION AGE PUBLISHING, INC.
Charlotte, NC • www.infoagepub.com

Library of Congress Cataloging-in-Publication Data

CIP record for this book is available from the Library of Congress
http://www.loc.gov

ISBNs: 979-8-88730-556-1 (Paperback)

   979-8-88730-557-8 (Hardcover)

   979-8-88730-558-5 (EPDF)

   978-1-83708-572-9 (EPUB)

Copyright © 2025 Information Age Publishing Inc.

All rights reserved. No part of this publication may be reproduced, stored in a retrieval system, or transmitted, in any form or by any means, electronic, mechanical, photocopying, microfilming, recording or otherwise, without written permission from the publisher.

Printed in the United States of America

DEDICATION

This poem is dedicated to all of the young people who afforded me the opportunity to work alongside them. To the public who attended their art exhibitions. To the teachers, school leaders, families, and community members who supported this important work. To those who supported me throughout this journey. I wrote this for you: To serve you…. You are powerful. Injustices overcome. You have prevailed. Each of you inspire people to walk alongside you. To take action. To rise up. To be present. To emerge from darkness. And … radiate into the heart, mind, and spirit of those who have the privilege to know you

To serve you…
You are powerful.
Injustices overcome.
You have prevailed.
Each of you inspire people to walk alongside you.
To take action.
To rise up.
To be present.
To emerge from darkness.
And…
Radiate into our hearts, minds, and spirits.

CONTENTS

1. Constructing Meaning
   Christa Boske *1*

2. Peace
   Ichgok *15*

3. Rainbow
   Nerds *25*

4. Life's Journey
   Ichgo *33*

5. Spirit
   TJ *41*

6. Hiraeth
   Q *49*

7. Family Love
   J *55*

8. Darkness Falling
   Kano *63*

9. All Equal
   Nitro *71*

10. Alexithymia
    T1 .... *81*

11. Spirituality
   DL 93

12. Trauma
   T2 103

13. Black Lives Matter Should Matter to Everyone
   Moneyback King 115

14. Conscious-Based Artmaking
   Christa Boske 127

About the Author 131

CHAPTER 1

CONSTRUCTING MEANING

Christa Boske

Artmaking provides spaces for learners to foster connections among mind, body, spirit, and lived experiences. I was invited to work alongside these learners, teachers, staff, and school leader to design spaces in which learners ask questions, engage in courageous dialogue, and connect with others. Youth expressed their frustration toward traditional rote memory; being isolated by their peers and community; and yearning for creativity and self-expression. This artmaking process seemed to provide spaces for self-expression and visualizing their understandings of justice (see Feinstein, 1985). They suggested artmaking offered alternative pathways to understanding complex content as well as spaces to look withing. These young artists discovered what mattered. They experienced this through self-reflection, research, and building community (see Serig, 2006). Together, youth concluded their artmaking constructed meaning and symbolic forms of their self-expression (see Anderson & Milbrandt, 2005).

One of the many challenges these authors faced centered on feeling alone, being excluded. They hoped their artmaking may bring awareness to "real" injustices, such as racism, poverty, mental health, abuse, and other injustices. Providing young artists with opportunities to engage in this transformational process often left them feeling authentically connected, empowered, and poised for action. This artmaking process did not dictate what to do; rather, artmaking made a significant difference in their sense of self connecting their senses, body, mind, and spirit. Their art was *felt*, and *lived*.

These authors emphasized the extent this artmaking provided them with spiritual connections essential to understanding themselves and others. The process of thinking about justice, empowerment, and advocacy provided them with an inner peace and calmness while engaging in this significant work. Their first-tellings of injustice lived within their bodies and translated into their artmaking. For many of these artists, artmaking may become a lifelong process that not only permeates their minds, but also their bodies. For many of these authors, this artmaking was the first time they were provided with safe spaces to utilize expressive arts to illustrate their understandings, power, and sense of control. Throughout this process, an overall harmony emerged among these artists in their learning spaces. They engaged in meaningful discussions with their school community members as their artmaking moved and spoke to them. Artists recognized their artmaking increased their awareness of self, who they are, and what they believe (see Anderson & Milbrandt, 2005).

This was the first time these artists engaged in artmaking to develop their capacity to critically think about and grapple with social justice issues important to them. They researched significant topics ranging from diversity to power to privilege to responsible citizens to activism to challenging systemic issues influencing their communities. This artmaking provided spaces for artists to illustrate what it means to live their lives through powerful visualized and textualized processes. They came to understand there is not one "correct" response; rather, their first-tellings, ways of knowing and being, are what matter most throughout their artmaking.

The general public was asked on a voluntary basis to document their insights regarding the justice exhibition on anonymous comment cards. Here's what the attendees had to say:

> *"Two things that stood out to me that people should learn: (1) Listen to children just like you do your peers. Age doesn't matter; (2) Art is necessary everywhere for healing, self-expression, learning and communication."*

> *"Some of the most powerful stories I've ever read in a long time and experiences that you wish no one would want any child to go through. Yet, seeing the way in which these youth chose to express themselves gave me a ton of hope for their future and the future of society. It gave me a feeling that they digested, understood, and processed these things through and look forward to a fulfilling future using art and their voices."*

> *"This art exhibition is very impressive. The children showed how they think about the world and chose to be vulnerable. I hope lessons are learned by everyone who experiences their art."*

> *"I'm amazed at this art. I am amazed at how brave these artists were to share their powerful truths. It takes a lot of courage and personal growth to be able to be that expressive and open. Amazing! The advice they give was very insightful. As an edu-*

cator, I agree that there should be more outlets like art for kids to explore themselves. Teachers, and people as a whole, need to be more patient with each other and understanding of everyone's unique life experiences. Thank you so much for sharing your art with the world."

"The art is moving, but once you read these stories, you see a person, a human being behind a behavior, an attitude and it's so important for us to see!"

"I am thankful for this program the youth participated in and to see how these young artists have been able to develop their art and tell their own stories because each and every person has an important story to tell, to share with the world. I am blown away learning about these young people's experiences and how they feel about their artwork. So much thought and effort went into every piece. I also appreciate the opportunity for them to give frank honest advice to teachers and schools. Fabulously done!"

"Art is expression and humans, especially youth, need to be heard and seen. Thank you for affording them with spaces to be heard and seen. These kids are amazing and strong!"

"I am feeling grateful for being able to attend this exhibition today as a 30 year old small business owner. As a female in the service industry as a cosmetologist, I think of my youth and how are and cosmetology, both were areas I felt I connected most and adults at that time discouraging my interest in pursuing art or cosmetology! I had a very troubled youth and art and beauty kept me stable and helped me to feel useful. I think that youth require artistic expression to grow and they can teach adults a lot. There were two pieces that anger was mentioned and sadly, I too felt a lot of that when I was younger and it has taken a lot of time to find a balance. These pieces spoke of that anger and sadness and it was a release for these youth, the feeling of being unloved or unloveable. My heart goes out to these young artists and I see the power in your messages-from one artist to another."

"This collection of art should be on permanent display in a gallery. It shows creativity, depth, power, awareness, and spirit of our youth. It gives us hope for the future of this younger generation."

"I came here not knowing what to expect. Wow! I loved all the paintings. This place is awesome. It was a friendly and cozy and pleasant atmosphere. I enjoyed talking to people about this work."

"Moving exhibition! Eye opening. Working through challenges through art. It was captivating and moved me."

"This is very powerful and disturbing at times because I had no idea youth thought about any of this or experienced things like racism. It was enlightening as well. Their stories are trasic, moving, and an expression of hope for our future."

"My breath has been taken away by everything I've seen today. I hope the artists continue to create no matter what!"

"I love the diverse display and the fact that I was able to learn about the artists. This doesn't happen at other exhibitions. We are normally limited to just knowing the name of the artist and the medium used. By scanning the QR codes I learned so much. I also loved the food and drink and how the chef created food that represented what the artists were saying. Everyone was so friendly! I just loved it!"

"This experience has been great. I enjoyed learning about social justice."

"Thank you so much to each and everyone of you who participated in this exhibit. It was amazing and moving. It made me really think and realize I need to do something about these issues."

"The art exhibit made me feel emotional, relatable, heard, understood, uncomfortable, sad ... and so many thoughts. When reading these abstracts, I found myself looking within and reflecting on my youth and what I had to deal with. Many of the stories were triggering and I started to think about how I still haven't fully healed. But now that I am in my 30s, I am ready to address these issues and heal these wounds. I appreciate the courage of these young artists and how they chose to display their art and share their messages with the world. This is a part of the process and it will continue to encourage them to use their voices, to realize they matter, and to speak up and do something about these injustices."

"All of the work was incredibly moving and gave me such insights into the lives of these artists. Their usage of shapes, lines, and color gave these pieces power. I really enjoyed being able to read about their creative processes and learn more about the techniques they all used to give their work their final form. Their stories are so important and foundational to this work. I look forward to attending more exhibitions and seeing their names in future galleries."

"It was powerful to see the combination of the great art and the words of the young artists who created it. So powerful!"

"The art exhibition is amazing. This expression of internal feelings and thoughts in the form of art provides an excellent way for young people to rehearse and share what is inside their hearts, but also displays talents they will continue to develop, explore, and nurture. Thank you for your dedication and belief in these young people and giving them spaces to share their voices."

"Reality in motion! This exhibit touched my spirit and I appreciate how this was an outlet for the youth and how they addressed justice issues."

"This exhibition is extremely important work! Not only can these stories be identifiable in that pieces remind you of your own life or the life of others you know and care about, but also, it gives you a voice to people who not only need to be heard, but know they matter! Their stories and art matter! Touching! Very supportive!"

"Very powerful! Very insightful! My heart goes out to these artists! I am impressed with the creativity demonstrated throughout this exhibition. These are stories EVERY educator should read/(need to) hear."

"Much gratitude for these beautiful expressions. The talent and depth of these works is breathtaking."

"I'm impresses with the level of though and emotion in each piece. The process in which youth have gone through to express themselves and what matters to them is simply amazing. What a valuable experience for them and those who attended this exhibition."

"Very impressive and impactful! I am coming back!"

"Some of these pieces were sad, but they were fascinating. My heart is proud for these young artists."

"This exhibit is so powerful and should be required for EVERY educator to experience. I feel so honored to have been able to experience this exhibition, read the stories, view the art, and their wonderful voices."

"Reading this as a Black teacher, I could definitely relate. These are stories I've heard in my family and amongst my friends 10 years ago. I'm frustrated that this didn't end with my generation. We deal with so much. You've dealt with so much, but still we fight every day to live. Just know that your are strong, young artists. I know every road is long. Take it day by day. But more importantly, thank you. Your art inspired me. Honestly, y'all had a grown man crying!! I need to live this work as you are living it."

"Absolutely moving. The depth of thought that went into these pieces is stunning. Thank you for being open and vulnerable and teaching us why this matters. Thank you for sharing your experiences and why we need to pay closer attention to these injustices. You are all so bright and your art and stories are so important to hear. Keep sharing. Keep making art. Keep living this work."

"As a Black man, the piece "Life and Death" is personal. It's like looking in a mirror. It speaks of the unique struggle of the Black man. This was amazing."

"Each piece of the art I saw today moved me. Your stories are real and were felt by each person who was told your story. Keep speaking, creating, and moving forward. You will continue to do great things and change the world one step at a time."

"There is so much thought and planning that went into this exhibition. The art work was amazing. The stories were captivating. Each work of art is stunning and you can tell the artists put lots of care into making them."

"After seeing and reading about your lives, so beautifully shared with your art, I felt like a big part of me has been reborn, reawakened to all that life has given to you at such an early age. This year, I promise all of you that I will learn life anew, that I will listen, that I will help make a positive difference in the lives of my students. I am a teacher. I am responsible for transforming myself. Thank you for this opportunity to learn from you and to be inspired by you."

"This exhibit truly was so powerful. Personally, I have not gone through many of these experiences or thought about these injustices, but I felt your work and your words. I felt your emotions. Thank you for sharing these personal parts of you through your art and words! It makes me want to use art to work through my own challenges. Thank you!"

"The students' artwork and emotional writings were very powerful. Many of the stories told can be related to students I work with. I look forward to trying this out and hope you will work with our students."

"This exhibit gave me more will power and need to things which highlight mental health to the parents. I speak to youth about healthy natural stress reduction techniques like focusing on positive thoughts through meditation, deep breathing, building positive relationships with the Creator, but adults need to learn this too, the sober way of health and how to spread love and peace. These art pieces and writings gave me stronger will power to spread the mental health to more youth, and the adults who often don't have it together in the their mind, heart, or spirit. I'm sending you all love who made this art."

"Such things should never happen to children. These injustices should never be in the face of youth. Many are seeking love, the basic foundation of society: security, safety, love, acceptance ... I feel that some of these youth need adults to protect them, to care, to love them, and to listen. These artists make it clear. We can no longer dismiss them or what matters to them. Thank you for sharing your art and stories with me."

"Artworks 1 and 2 were absolutely powerful! How transparent and courage to share their art and stories. I enjoyed reading these stories and value this experience. I am proud of all of you."

"These pieces of art were much deeper than I ever imagined. That's on me. I guess I don't often think young people think about these issues."

"The emotions and thought that went into this work is unbelievable. I am moved and very impressed with this work at this exhibition."

"This was extremely powerful and emotional for me. I was blown away by the insight and wisdom from such young people. This experience will stay with me as we continue to educate and allow students to fully express themselves about critical issues that affect them in their lives. Thank you for doing this work with young people and thank you for this experience."

"Very powerful works and words!" So great to see young people engaging in self-expression in its purest form. Keep changing the world! You changed me!"

"The piece Hiraeth moved me. Thoughts of a sacred home, safe from colonization. The warm safety of the African sun. This work speaks of that great place. Bravo!"

"It's really beautiful and inspiring to see their hearts and voices and perspectives tonight. It takes courage to share your story and it was a powerful experience to view each art work."

"Being able to transmute your experiences into art is so incredible. These stories are so deeply impactful in someone's life. It is so wonderful to see what this ability to express oneself has done for these young artists. It transformed them. They know they matter. How powerful for them!"

"My Thoughts: I thought these people are really good wrighters and artests. They are better than me and that's cool that there better and what you experience is always

better for the future! I was reading more about the art and I have more to say. Art is a thing that you can do if your angry or sad and you can get it out! I love art too and sometimes I do are when I want to get things out. It works. This was great."
—*11 year old*

"When i see the Art my heart feel uncomfortable And it is Like something pushing my heart. I Liked all of this art." —8 year old

Art became a means to look deeper within, understand oneself, and share their truth with others. Their artmaking provided diverse ways to communicate their lived experiences. It was an imaginative tool utilized to showcase how these young people navigated changing conditions and solved problems in order to assert oneself in meaningful ways. Their truth emerged (see Smoke, 1982). Together, they recognized themselves as *catalysts* seeking, promoting, and making meaningful change (see Boske, 2019).

Most expressed the need for viewers to feel their artmaking and *to be moved* to do something about these injustices. They were often transported to new spaces with an increased awareness of the unfamiliar. This artmaking emerged as a transformative experience, one in which they hoped would be afforded to all learners around the world. They concluded one of their responsibilities as young artists was to bring forth an emotional and physical response to their artmaking. Together, youth wanted their art to mitigate a strong sense of unity versus numbing, which they often experienced within their communities. These artists wanted their artmaking to motivate and inspire viewers to transform their thinking about injustices to addressing/interrupting these systemic oppressive practices by "doing."

Engaging in artmaking was not a solitary event. Artists worked together and shared spaces. They came together as a community to see the world in new ways (see Boske, 2014). They critically thought about the myriad of justice-oriented issues facing their communities and decided that sharing these understandings was worthwhile and pertinent to the process. Their capacity to accept and embrace one another was essential. Their sense of community became a source of inspiration, admiration, and cultivation. Together, they transcended narrowly defined ways of being, worldviews, and divisiveness within real world justice issues. As they moved forward through their artmaking, "rules" were challenged; they drew attention to the need for cultural adaption and considerations; and concluded "us vs. them" was not conducive to understanding the power of "we." As they reflected on their artmaking, these artists concluded their artmaking had the capacity to transform oneself, their communities, and ultimately, the possibility of meaningful world-wide change (see Boske, 2019). (See Figure 1.1).

Figure 1.1

Art Exhibition Opening to the General Public

Together, they provide readers with opportunities to reveal injustices often ignored by their schools and communities. Their artmaking created spaces to engage in meaningful dialogue regarding how they understood the influence of their lived experiences, their bodies, minds, thoughts, and responses to injustices. Artists recognized their artmaking as a collaborative to educate others, but more importantly, promoting cohesion and self-empowerment. For the first time, artists openly discussed, explored, and translated their first-tellings into artmaking. They dialogued about artmaking materials, composition, arrangement, and messaging. These artists carefully selected, processed, organized, and designed their artmaking to ensure their ideas were communicated through their artmaking (see Figure 1.2).

Authors began this process by documenting their ideas. The content of their first-tellings played a vital role with each artwork, which is critical to understanding their why society should pay close attention to these injustices. Their artmaking reflected their perceptions and responses to their lived experiences. In addition to the content, these artists also learned about the significance aesthetics plays to the look and feel of their artmaking. These artists came to understand aesthetics as a space to create their own knowledge, which moved beyond individual perceptions, and reflected on injustices facing their communities. Their artmaking reflects imagery that depicts their lived realities, values, and imaginative possibilities (see Figure 1.3).

Engaging in this innovative process that exemplified the need for self-expression played a significant role in their understanding of self. In other words, these artists utilized this experience as a means of making some-

Constructing Meaning 9

Figure 1.2

General Public Discussing the Impact of the Art

Figure 1.3

Attendees Reading the Art Abstracts Using QR Codes

thing new or evolving: their own transformation. These artists expressed the desire for additional opportunities to engage in making their own art versus scripted lessons and predetermined outcomes (see Figure 1.4).

Chapters in Review

All artists chose to use pseudonyms for each of their chapters. In Chapter 2, Ichgo shares her chapter "Peace" emphasizing how she makes

Figure 1.4

Community Member Attending an Opening

connections with nature, animals, and her family to navigate injustices she endures. Ichgo identifies the significance of her artmaking and the symbolism behind her artmaking. Nerds, the author of "Rainbow" in Chapter 3, explains how he navigated identifying as trans. He further explains how his artmaking directly aligns with his experiences in K–12 schools and what supports are needed. "Life's Journey," Chapter 4, which is the Ichgo's second contribution to this book and art exhibition, examines how her lived experiences shaped how she understands injustice. Ichgo utilized pathways and spaces to illustrate "forks in the road" and the extent her choices influenced her lived experiences. In Chapter 5, "Spirit," TJ guides the reader through her journey, illustrating the extent this artmaking provided her with sacred spaces to deepen her understanding of the injustices she lived. TJ's first-tellings provide us with the power love plays in developing a strong sense of self. The author Q, in Chapter 6, introduces the term "hiraeth" to her readers, which is the focus and title of this chapter. Q emphasizes as a young Black woman her yearning and longing for culturally responsive practices and policies in schools. This author stresses this sense of homesickness and distinct feeling of being lost in school due to the lack of authentic Black history, teachers, and respect for her community. In Chapter 7, J titled her chapter "Family Love." J clearly identifies injustices often faced by children who become part of the larger system after experiencing abuse. This author emphasizes the need for all children to have loving families. In J's artmaking, she creates her ideal family consisting of two parents and siblings. Kano, in Chapter 8 titled "Darkness Falling," utilizes his passion for comic book and video game characters to illustrate injustices facing children who live with domestic violence. He emphasizes the need many children feel to protect those they love and how often they feel helpless. Kano created his own video character and embedded his first poem about his lived experiences in his artmaking. In Chapter 9, Nitro shares information regarding racism and divisive practices implemented to perpetuate separateness among people. His chapter, titled "All Equal" provides readers with a deep understanding of his reflective process as he navigates White supremacy throughout his artmaking. T1, who authors "Alexithymia," Chapter 10, created several panels in her artmaking to immerse viewers in an emotional state. She created an ocean and feelings of drowning. T1 titled her art "Alexithymia" to illustrate the challenges of navigating and identifying her emotions. She contends this artmaking served as a release to the injustices she faces. In Chapter 11, DL in "Spirituality," the author created her artmaking to illustrate how she utilizes her higher power to bring light to the darkness she lives. The injustices DL faces will not overcome her spirit. "Trauma" is the title of Chapter 12 and authored by T2. This author engaged in artmaking for the first time and discusses how she embedded herself in her artmaking as a means to reflect, process, and foster courageous conversations.

Moneyback King, the author of Chapter 13 titled "Black Lives Matter Should Matter to Everyone," created his first painting/drawing utilizing his raps, research, and first-tellings. As a young biracial artist, he emphasizes how his lived experiences and those of his community must be recognized and celebrated. In Chapter 14, I draw conclusions from the authors' artmaking. I emphasize the need to provide learners with spaces to give themselves permission to be creative, utilize artmaking to understand both micro/macro systems, and centering ourselves through authentic justice-oriented artmaking (see Figure 1.5).

Artists suggest this artmaking process often helped them focus their attention, when oftentimes, they struggled with centering themselves. Their authentic engagement seemed to increase their cognitive capacity as well as improve their capacity to connect with others. Their artmaking was a creative offering to deepen their understanding of justice, their capacity to contribute to something larger than themselves, and develop a stronger sense of self. Their lived experiences seemed directly correlated with the justice issues they believed were most relevant to making meaningful change in their communities. Ultimately, their imaginary possibilities often drove their creativity, innovation, and commitment to this work (see Figure 1.6).

These artists are convinced this artmaking process brought them together in new ways to share and discuss what matters most to them. As they encountered their artmaking as individuals and as a vital member of a group, they expanded on their notions of "we." Together, they began to

Figure 1.5

Family Discussing the Public Art During the Exhibition

Figure 1.6

Meaningful Conversations About the Artmaking

understand their new ways of knowing contained real world consequences. For example, they examined voting rights as well as voter suppression deepening their understanding of White-washing history. These discussions brought them together to share and discuss their lived experiences. As they engaged in this artmaking, they became more understanding of others as well as the role artmaking plays to encourage inclusive practices and embracing differences (see Figure 1.7).

Figure 1.7

DJ Playing Music While Attendees from the General Public Dialogue About the Artmaking at the Exhibition

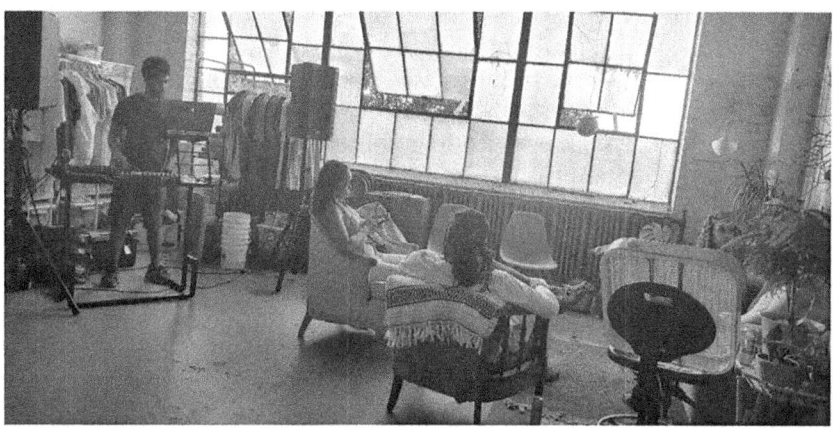

As artists engaged in this artmaking, they expanded their understandings from "me" to "we." Throughout this process, artists invited others into conversations about poverty, marginalization, segregation, global warming, the need for clean water, racism, mental health, and other social/political/ecological issues (see Figure 1.8).

Figure 1.8

Attendees Discussing the Artmaking

The power to create, freedom to express oneself, and space to contribute to something larger than oneself seemed to ignite their sense of wonderment. These new understandings afforded artists opportunities to shift perspectives of self and others. As they engaged in this work, these artists concluded their art and thoughts had the capacity to transform injustice into experiences for meaningful change. Their artmaking uplifted their spirits, sense of self, and increased awareness of their power to make meaningful change. In other words, they realized they mattered. Artists recognized their artmaking encouraged them to think and move beyond their perceived limitations.

REFERENCES

Anderson, T., & Milbrandt, M. K. (2005). *Art for life: Authentic instruction in art*. McGraw-Hill.

Boske, C. (2014). Critical reflective practices: Connecting to social justice. In I. Bogotch & C. Shields (Eds.), *International handbook of social [in]justice and educational leadership* (pp. 289–308). Springer.

Boske, C. (2019). *Standing still is not an option: School children using art for social change*. Information Age Publishing.

Feinstein, H. (1985). Art as visual metaphor. *Art Education*, *38*(4), 26–29.

Serig, D. (2006). A conceptual structure of visual metaphor. *Studies in Art Education*, *47*(3), 229–247.

CHAPTER 2

PEACE

Ichgo (Elizabeth)

I have anger issues. I want peace for me and for everyone. I have to work on my anger. I was being physically aggressive. It's been like that for a while. I don't remember when it started. I don't know why I am so angry.

School was hard for me. I didn't want to do my homework and stuff. I was very quiet. I stopped wanting to do my work in 5th grade. It was the teachers. They just didn't help me. I did ask for help. They just didn't help me the way I needed. My mom and my stepdad tried to help me. I just didn't want to do my work (see Figure 2.1).

Figure 2.1

Some People Who Attended One of Our Openings

16 ICHGO (ELIZABETH)

I was physically aggressive at home. It started around 5th grade. I was punching things like in my room. It helped me calm down. I used my punching bag. Since then, I have been learning how to deal with my anger. I spend time with my animals. I have four horses, three cats, and two dogs. My horses are Zach, Illy, Mai Tai, and Asirrah. They are 30, 17, 14, and 9 years old. I don't know how long they live. I am smiling right now. I grew up with them, so they are like my comfort animals, I guess because I grew up with them. They provide me love and they are always there for me, no matter what. They let me be around them and love on them as well and they love on me. I ride them. I guess cause my mom and my grandma rides horses. So, I learned from them (see Figure 2.1).

Figure 2.1

More People From the Public Learning About Our Activism

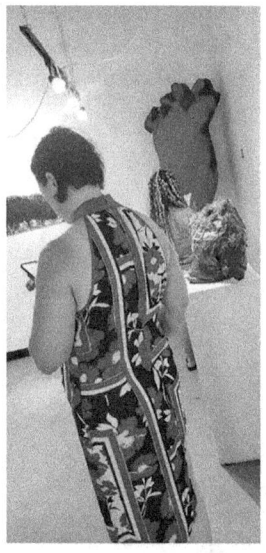

Me and my mom take care of the horses. They are on our property. My three cats are Clover, Binx, and Mischief. Clover is around 9 ... Binx is almost three and Mischief. They give me comfort. They are always there for me as well. They are loyal. I mean, they are always there and will not betray me in any shape or form. The whole family takes care of them. That's my brother, little sister, my mom, stepdad and me. My dogs are Dixie. She's 11. Tyson is the other dog. He is 12 weeks old. He is a boxer and lab mix. I mean, they give me exercise because I am always chasing the puppy around. They give me protection. They give me happiness.

I felt betrayed .
I want to feel protected.
I want someone there for me…
Always
When my animals are with me,
I feel happy.
I find the most happiness with them.
That's because
I grew up with them
They are my safe place.
When everything went downhill,
They were there.
Along with my mom.
My mom
Even through the hard times,
She was there.
She gave us shelter,
Food, and supported us.
Even if she didn't like our decision,
She still supported us.
I felt loved,
You know.
That's peace.
It's what everyone should have.
It's what I want for myself
And everyone.

This was my first poem. It's cool. I smiled just now.

My Art

I made my body out of box tape and paper towel and modpodge. I had someone wrap my body with box tape and first I had on plastic. It looked like a big plastic bag. You put that on first and then you put the box tape on there. You gotta make sure the tape covers everything. After we put the tape on my body then we had to cut it off. We made a cut in the back and pulled it off. That was the easy part.

I decided to make my body my art. It's like your body helps you a lot and gives you a lot of support. It helps you stand, walk, breath, and tries its hardest to heal our wounds. Not just wounds on the outside, but on the inside, like someone hurting you. I made my body because it's powerful. My body helps me heal. I want to feel peace inside (see Figure 2.4).

I do find peace. I felt peaceful when I did this art. I also feel that way when I go to sleep. Personally, I have a weighted blanket. So, when I was

Figure 2.3

Making My Body and Portraying Animals as Bringing Peace

Figure 2.4

More Animals

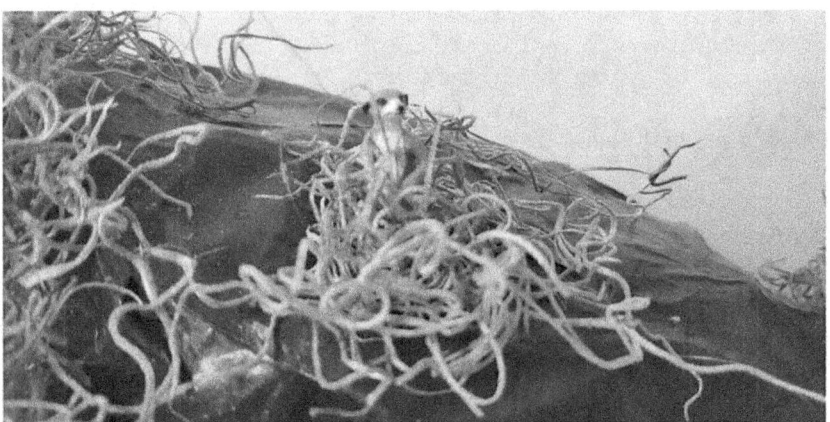

taped up, you know ... my body ... it felt like a hug. It was a good feeling. The last time I had a hug, I hugged my mom at the house, which was five days ago. I not much of a touchy person. I don't really need hugs every day. Not sure why but I just don't. Maybe someday I will but not now.

I covered my body with paper towel that was brown and modpodge. You have to tear the paper towel into pieces and then you can rub it in modpodge or you can put modpodge on the body or you can dip it in the modpodge and put it on the body and use a brush to keep it on there. I did all of them. It just depended on the mood I was in (see Figure 2.5).

Figure 2.5.

My Art on a Pedestal

I decided to paint my body red. I painted my body red. That represents my anger. It's red all over. When I am angry, I get tense. I painted it red to show my anger inside. I have a lot of anger inside. Sometimes I just fight people. I don't always know why. I just know I have anger issues.

I wanted a little family on my art. I had a family of little people in a bag. I chose to put a family of five on my shoulder. I put them in the order I did because it represents my family. I know my family has my back. I hot glued them to my shoulder. They are standing there on my shoulder because they give me strength. I also put moss around them. This is real moss. It is cool. The moss around them represents this barrier they make for me to protect me against the world. They shield me. They can't always shield me because I am going to get hurt but I know they do what they can for me. They protect me (see Figure 2.6).

I also had a bag of animals I wanted. I chose to put animals on there. I put the animals on my body. I hot glued them too. Animals, well, I love them. They are my biggest support, my comfort. I love animals. They are my friends. I talk to them. I put moss around them too. It's to represent protection as well. They protect me.

Figure 2.6

My Family

I painted a peace sign on my chest. I painted it so the colors came together and mixed with each other. This represents different parts of me. I want peace inside. I want the different parts of me to have peace. I painted it on my chest because I want you to see it's a big part of me and it is in my heart (see Figure 2.7).

Figure 2.7.

Finding Peace

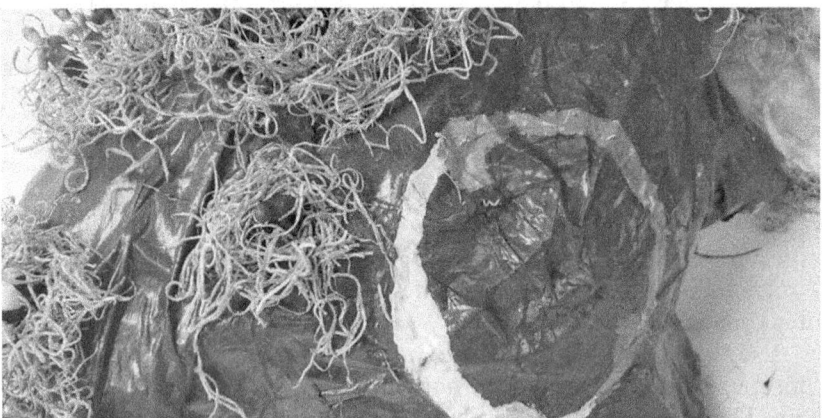

I have real moss coming out of my neck. This is showing growth of my mind. It is about getting my mental health stronger. I am trying to grow and change. I don't want to always be angry. I think everyone should have peace inside of them. That is something I want for every person (see Figure 2.8).

Figure 2.8

The Public Viewing My Artmaking

When I finished my art, I felt happy because I like doing art. I never did anything like this before. It felt weird because it's about me and I usually do artwork that is abstract and it's not specific. It felt different. It was something new (see Figure 2.9).

I felt free to do what I wanted to do. I didn't need to ask if it was okay. It was okay to do. I put a lot of thinking into this art. I normally don't do that when I am doing art. It was very cool. I felt good after I finished it. I would do this again.

Profits from my art went to an animal shelter because animals make a difference in this world, especially to me (see Figure 2.10).

I don't think teachers and principals should give all this homework. They need to go over things. When that doesn't happen, I feel frustrated and angry. I got angry in school. School was hard for me. Kids need time to let go. They need time to think and do art. Sometimes we don't know what to say … or how to say it. When I did this art, it just came to me. It was cool.

Figure 2.9

One of the Art Galleries Featuring Our Artmaking

Figure 2.10

My Art in a Gallery

Art should be in school, and we should have more art in classes and more classes to do art. Cause a lot of kids really like it. It is an outlet to our emotions. We need to be able to express how we feel about school or what we are learning or about what's goin' on … or anything that we are thinking. Teachers and principals should want to know what's going on with us. If they care, then they would ask us or show us that they care. They should ask us every day how we are feeling. And if we don't have it, you can explode. That is what we are trying to avoid … exploding.

We don't want that. If teachers could give us more art to do and let us do what we want to do, then kids might be able to do good in school. I never experienced anything like this in school. I was never asked what I thought about anything I was learning or what I wanted to learn more about. I never got to talk about my life or what was going on … and I don't think teachers really cared. If you don't know me, then how do you think I am going to learn? Do you even care about what I am thinking? Do you care about how I feel? Don't think we are learning when you don't even know my name … or my family … or ask how I am doing. It won't happen. Doing this art was important to me. I go to share what I don't talk about … I felt like someone cared about me. Why did I have to wait until now? Don't you think that's too long to wait? I do.

All I know is how I felt doing this art and working through what matters to me. I know I was feeling peace inside when I did this. I know I felt like people actually cared. I think every kid should be able to do this kind of art in school. It was cool. I learned a lot about me and what's important to me.

CHAPTER 3

RAINBOW

Jadyn [Nerds]

My social justice art is about the LGBTQ community. Why? I identify as trans. I have been known I was trans since I was able to form sentences. I was little. I don't know how I knew I was in the wrong body. I just knew. Something told me I wasn't the same person people saw me as. Somehow, I knew I had the heart and brain of a guy, but I was born a girl. Don't ask me how. I just knew. It's kinda like someone asking a straight boy why he likes girls. He just knows. It's the same thing (see Figure 3.1).

Figure 3.1

The Public Viewing My Artmaking

My mom says she is fine with it. I feel supported by her. I did come out to my best friend when I was 11. I trusted my friend more than my family. I just knew they accepted me for me. I didn't have to act a certain way. My best friend and I were friends since kindergarten. That's a long time. He has always been nice to me. I felt safe coming out to him. I knew him for a long time. I thought, "Why would he flip flop?" I knew he wouldn't. And he didn't (see Figure 3.2).

Figure 3.2

Reading My Work

My principal knows too. But, I didn't tell that person. The hospital told the principal. I was in the hospital dealing with some things. When I got back to school, he met with me. I think he met with me because it was the end of the year. I was in getting ready to go into my first year in high school. The principal asked if he needed to tell the high school teachers anything. I said no. I don't think they need to know anything about me being trans. Everyone has been nice to me and accepted me so far. I know that isn't like that for other kids who are trans. A lot of trans kids have a hard time. Their families can be mean. People at school can be mean. That didn't happen to me though. Everyone was cool (see Figure 3.3).

The principal was already about to tell the high school teachers my pronouns and stuff. I go by he/him. I will probably tell them myself the more I think about it. It will be awkward though … because 8th grade science … well, it was my first period of the day. And once I got back from the last

Figure 3.3

My Art

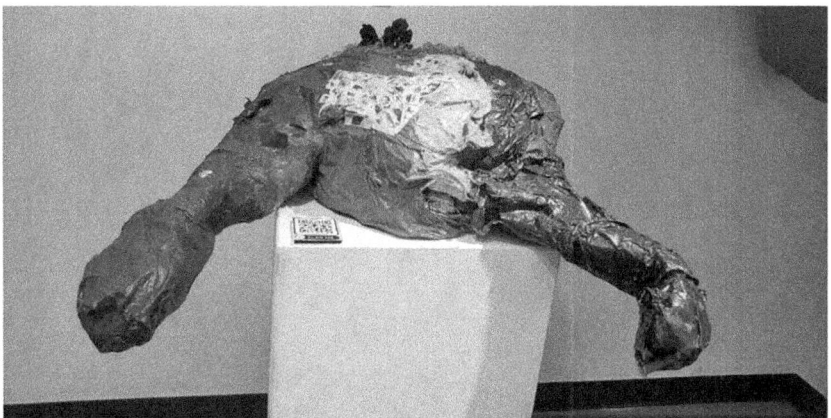

residential I was at, on the second day, she pulled me, and said, "I know your pronouns are he and him." The teacher asked if I wanted to sit with the guys I was close to. I said yeah … because we get to goof off. Students have been cool. I have been with these students since kindergarten. We are tight group.

My Art

I wanted to do something about me being trans. I decided to make my body. I made a cast of my body out of box tape. It was pretty cool. I never did anything like that before. One of the other students helped me and I helped that student too. We learned how to use the box tape and wrap our bodies. I did my upper body, but not my head, but did my arms and hands too. I stood still for a long time while another student wrapped my body. When she was done, she used scissors to cut the cast so I could slide it off of me. The hands were the most difficult because they got stuck a few times. We laughed taking it off of me (see Figure 3.4).

I made my arms out because I wanted to welcome people. I wanted people to welcome me … and other trans kids. It's like giving us a hug. I want people to embrace and accept everyone. It doesn't have to not just be people in the LGBTQ community.

I decided to paint a rainbow on my body. I used red, made orange with yellow and red…had green … blue … and made purple a few times until I got the color I wanted … I made it using red and blue. The rainbow …

Figure 3.4

My Art at Another Public Art Gallery

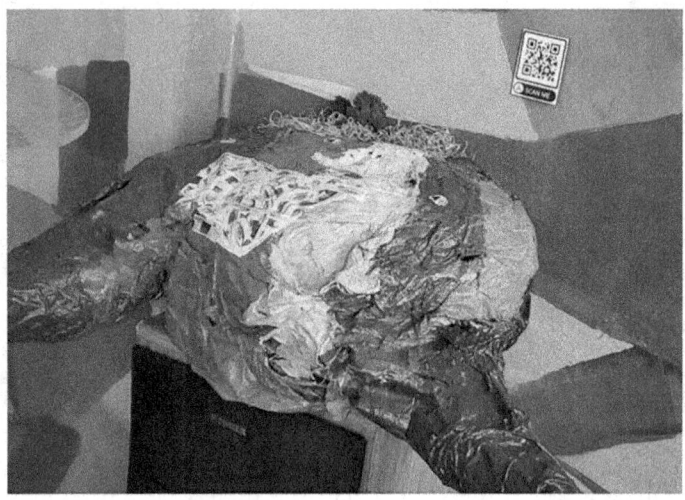

uh ... it's the universal sign for gay people ... when you see a rainbow flag or sign ... most everyone know it means that person is part of the LGBTQ community. Rainbows are also a sign of happiness. I like that the rainbow is a sign for being gay. It's pride month. Did you know? It's June ... the whole month.

I also wanted to tell people that anyone who is trans or gay or part of the LGBTQ community wants to be seen and heard. I thought about what represents being seen. And what I mean by that is having people actually see you for who you are, not for what they want you to be or who to love or how to dress or how to identify ... so, I decided to use eyes to represent being seen. I found eyeballs when I searched on the internet. I want people to be seen. I want people to be fully seen for who they are. It's important. When people are seen, they feel important ... accepted ... you know, for who they are. They don't have to be something they're not. I cut out a lot of eyes. I decided to make a heart and put it in the middle of my chest. I mod podged them into the shape of a heart because everyone deserves love and should be able to love who they want, right? (see Figure 3.5).

I wanted to make sure people are heard. I thought about how to represent that. I decided to use the sound symbol that you might see. I sent those to my teacher and the teacher printed those out for me too. I want everyone, not just LGBTQ, to be heard and their opinions heard so they don't feel left out. It feels good to be heard (see Figure 3.6).

Rainbow 29

Figure 3.5

My Heart

Figure 3.6

Can You Hear Me Now?

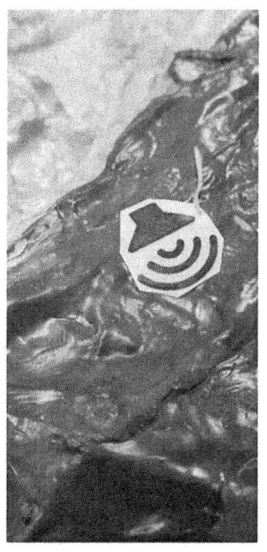

The back is painted black to symbolize the people who are in the closet and hiding their sexual orientation and gender identity. Sexual orientation is who you are attracted to … like if you were a cisgender person, you would say you were straight like cisgender female. Cis is like you are okay with the gender you were born as … you are okay … you don't have that gut feeling you are in the wrong body. Gender identity is if you were to have a driver's license, it says physical features like brown hair and brown eyes, but it also says the gender. It says like male or female. And what that means is that how you identify. It's how you wish to be seen.

I put moss in my body and I have a tree I hot glued in there. It represents how the LGBTQ community has grown to be a part of our world. People to be accepted and heard … and seen (see Figure 3.7).

Figure 3.7

The Heart

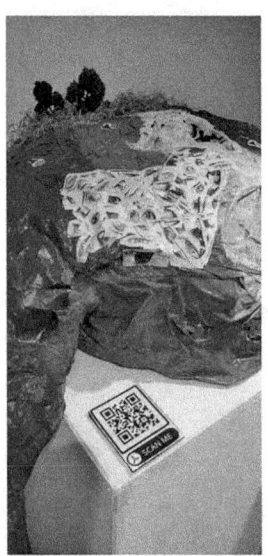

I was taped up to make my body cast. It was hot and sticky, but for the most part, it was a lot of work. I had to cut the cast off of my body. And then I had to put mod podge on every piece of paper towel. I had to tear the paper towel and then make sure I got it full of mod podge. The I put the paper towel with mod podge on the body. It was really messy. I used a brush and brushed more mod podge on there. I didn't think it would ever dry. It did. I didn't think it would be clear either. But it was. It just takes a long time to mod podge. You have to have patience. I don't really have that.

This art taught me that. You have to be patient and slow. This stuff takes time. You have to think about the details and ask yourself a lot of questions about why you do this ... what does this mean ... why that color ... you get the picture. Everything means something. That is cool.

The mod podge wouldn't dry as fast as I wanted it to. I had to use a hair dryer sometimes to help it go faster. I got really frustrated sometimes. I wanted everything to be done so I could start painting. I had to let it dry overnight.

When it dried then I got to paint. I had to do the little paint stuff, so the paint kept mixing, so I would get frustrated. I made my own colors like purple and orange. I made the colors of the rainbow because I was doing the LGBTQ community. I wanted people to see the rainbow colors and know it was about LGBTQ.

But in the end, I like the outcome. I like that I mean I didn't see it going anywhere ... I never did anything like this before so I didn't know if it would even turn out ... but I like it ... I was talking to my mom, and she said she will come to the gallery and check it out (see Figure 3.8).

Figure 3.8

My Art in One Gallery

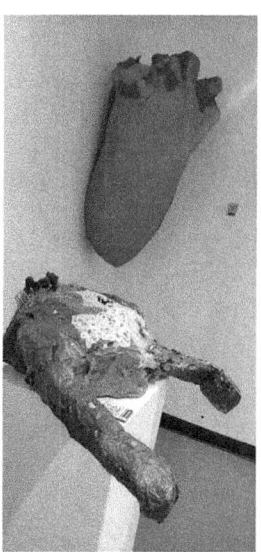

I mean it's really cool that it's in a gallery. I do art, so it's like my beginning. I hope to help people with my art and with the money to help other kids. I didn't think this was possible, but I did it. I quit so many times ... or

I needed a break ... I wasn't very patient ... I learned I need to be patient ... can't have everything right now ... and that is very true with my art. And now, I have motivation. Once I started seeing it painted and finishing it ... it was something I would like to do again. Not the same thing. I want to do something different. I feel like anyone with ideas like this, you should pursue it, because it may turn out in a museum.

This gave me a chance to talk about being trans. I want to help people understand. I hope my art helps.

Profits from my artmaking went to the Trevor Project. Check it out at https://www.thetrevorproject.org/

Advice

I feel like teachers and principals need to let this happen. They need to bring more art into schools. It can't just be in art class. Not everyone has art anyway. When I did this, I was free. I could do anything I wanted to do. I had freedom to make choices and share what I wanted to talk about. Kids need this.

It is not their life to be controlled. Kids think about things too. We don't really get a chance to talk about what is on our minds. It's our lives. We need to live our lives. We don't need people hovering over us every day of the week telling us we should be this ... don't be that ... be this. We want freedom and can do things by ourselves.

This art gave me freedom to express myself. It's been on my mind ... the trans situation. It felt good to release it. I felt like people listened this time.

There's always a back story. Teachers and principals need to know students' back stories. If you don't know how then you need to learn how. They should teach you this when you are in college. You need to know how to talk to kids ... to work with them ... and do things that mean something to them. You can learn about the kids through their art. I just don't remember this ever happening to me in school until now. This was a cool experience. My art is in a gallery and people are going to learn from it.

CHAPTER 4

LIFE'S JOURNEY

Ichgo

I made two pieces for this. I made another cast of my body. I wanted to focus on my life's journey. I want people to learn from my life. My life is colorful, but it is not perfect. Life is not perfect. My life has times where I did good and times I didn't do as well. I wanted to show that (see Figures 4.1 and 4.2).

Figures 4.1 and 4.2

Pathways, Choices, and Growth

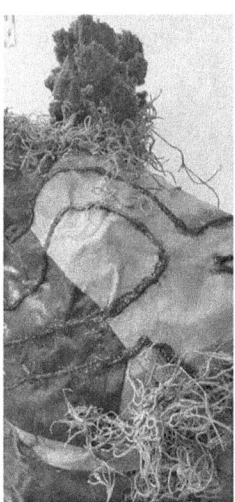 

34   JADYN [NERDS]

I put different colors on there because life is colorful and can be amazing. In my life, my family and my animals and my friends are amazing. They are like patches. These patches are like my life. I have different experiences and they all come together and make me who I am (see Figure 4.3).

Figure 4.3

Up Close

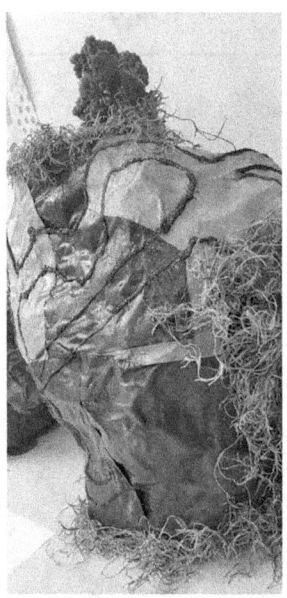

I put fabric on my body because fabric can make many different things. Fabric can be used for different things like clothes or blankets or anything really. That's like me. Each fabric is like a different part of me. When I put all of these together you have me. I mod podged these fabric pieces on my body. I put a bunch of mod podge on the body and then I put the fabric down. I put more mod podge on my brush and brushed it on the fabric. This made it stick better. When it dries, you can't see it. It is hard and keeps the fabric on. It's kinda like life. I had to deal with different things. They weren't going away. I had to be strong too (see Figures 4.4 & 4.5).

I asked for glitter. I wanted to make lines on my body like roads. I wanted them out of glitter ... brown ... l ike a road. I decided to put roads all over on my body. These are the different paths we choose in life. Sometimes we have bumps in the road. Sometimes we don't. Sometimes we have to choose which way we want to go. I put the roads on my body to represent

Figure 4.4

A Person is Reading My Abstract on His Phone

Figure 4.5

Someone is Reading About My Art

this. They go across my body. Some connect and some don't. That's like life. Sometimes we go on another path ... sometimes we get stuck ... sometimes the path doesn't go anywhere and we are lost. These roads are made of glitter because life is messy. Glitter is messy. But it also can be shiny. But when life shines, like glitter, you can still shine too ... even though life is sucky (see Figure 4.6).

Figure 4.6

Trees Symbolize Growth

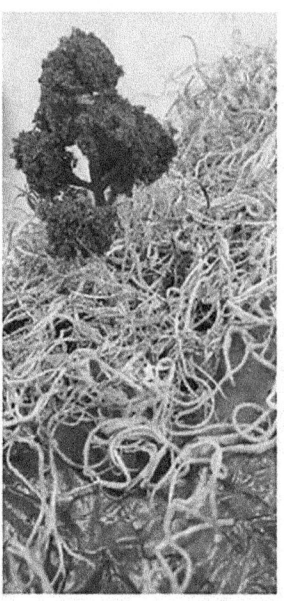

I added moss everywhere to my body. I hot glued it on. I did that to show you can still grow even though things might be tough. To me moss represents life and growth. We need to keep growing (see Figure 4.7).

I put three trees on top of my body. I hot glued them on. Not every tree is the same, so it's like knowing nobody is the same, but we are growing. We just don't all grow the same way. That's okay. But we need to grow. Everyone does. And all trees have roots. These are like your supports ... the roots ... they hold you in the ground so you can stand ... so you can see ... and if the wind comes, you don't fall down because you have roots ... these roots hold you. These trees have roots that represent people who love and care about you. They help you grow too. This is just like the moss around the trees (see Figure 4.8).

Figure 4.7

People Came to the First Exhibition to Learn More About What Injustices We Want People to Deal With

Figure 4.8

My Art Is on Display at a Gallery

38 JADYN [NERDS]

Everyone grows in different places during their life. Sometimes it takes longer for people to find their way, than others. But we are all on a path. We all need people that care about us. There is always going to be one person in the world who cares about you, but you may just not know it (see Figure 4.9).

I wasn't able to talk about this stuff this way without doing this art. Doing this art really helped me. It helped me think about my life and what I wanted people to learn about me … about life so they can grow too. And, I learned how much people really care (see Figure 4.10).

We need more of this art in school. I never did anything like this before. Everything had a reason for being on my art … the fabric … mod podge … moss … glitter … it was cool to do. I would do this again.

Figure 4.9

My Art at the Second Exhibition

Figure 4.10

The Public Reading My Abstract

CHAPTER 5

SPIRIT

Tessa [TJ]

Sometimes you have to make your own family because the people you depend on can't be depended on. You have to make your own family. This is my justice issue. Every child deserves to have a family and be loved and be accepted for who they are. Kids should never have to grow up in the system. Everyone needs a family. Everyone needs love. That is what this is about … my art. Even your own family might drop you in a heartbeat (see Figure 5.1).

Figure 5.1

People Reading My Abstract During an Art Gallery Opening

42 TESSA [TJ]

My art is about the value of family. Family is like something that I never had. It was ripped away from me. My motto is "build your own family." My biological family is just a mess. Trying to tell people that even if you don't have your own family, you can build your own family. I just had this chance yesterday to have my own family and it was ripped away from me. My mom gave her crazy boyfriend custody of me. I was balling my eyes out because this was the worst possible thing. And yesterday, I lost a baby. My mom ripped that from me. She would not allow me to keep my baby, so … and the baby's father is being difficult right now and I don't need him to be difficult. He is not communicating with me whatsoever (see Figure 5.2).

Figure 5.2

My Artmaking at the Second Art Exhibition

My parents gave me plan B, which is like a pill version of getting rid of a baby. So, it didn't work. And, fast forward to the next month, I actually miscarried a baby and it all came out. So, fast forward to another weekend, I was put on birth control. I found out my mom was lying to me and getting a shot for birth control. I said I would get it even though I said I didn't want it. I just wanted someone to love. I wanted someone to love me (see Figure 5.3).

I wanted to meet my mom in the middle, and my mom let her boyfriend make a decision about me. A very personal decision. Because I stood up for myself, they decided to put me down even more … they continue to say and call me things like:

Figure 5.3

People From the Public Discussing My Art

trifling
nasty
for getting pregnant
embarrassment to the family
I felt hurt
I felt my world was collapsing in on me.
They don't want anything to do with me.

Luckily, I have my best friend with me by my side and I'm just taking it day by day now. I'm okay now. I was able to talk about this … and I did it in my art … and then I changed my art when I started to think about all of this. It changed what I wanted to do. I thought about it different. I ended up making art about my future and what I want for me and for my future child or family that I make.

My Art

At first, I wanted to make a womb. It represented life and love and family. I thought that's where it all starts … so I wanted to make a womb … but I didn't know what that looked like. We found some pictures online and I decided to make one. I used pieces of cloth, three balloons and mod podge. I blew up the balloons. One of them popped. I used box tape to tape the balloons together. After that I used the fabric and painted mod podge on the balloons. I put more mod podge on the balloons. Then I put the pieces of cloth on there. I used a flower pattern. I wanted it to be soft like love. It took a day to dry. I tried to use a hair dryer to make it dry faster. That worked.

I found some red cloth. I wanted to make a heart out of paper towel and cover it with red cloth. That was hard. I put the paper towel and red fabric in the mod podge. There was a lot of it. Then I started to make the paper towel into the shape of a heart by twisting the long piece. I got frustrated because I didn't know how to do it the way I saw it in my head. I asked for help. We did it together and then I finished it. After that I covered it with red fabric. The fabric was big. I wanted to cover the whole heart. I had to make sure the paper towel and the red cloth was really covered with mod podge. It was very very messy. I had it all over my hands. I had to let it dry overnight. I didn't think all of the white mod podge would be clear, but it was the next day. I liked the way it turned out. That was what I thought about. Now I had a heart. I was going to put that on the inside of the womb. I would need to cut a hole in the womb and put the heart on the inside. I ended up changing my mind in the end (see Figure 5.4).

Figure 5.4

My Heart

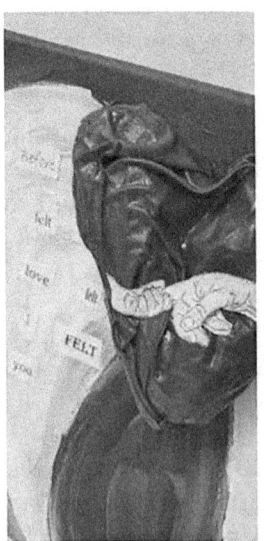

I started with the idea of making a womb. The fabric had a soft pattern with little flowers on it and it was blue. I used fabric to show this is loving and soft ... inside the womb I wanted heartbeat photos covering the inside ... and then I wanted my voice coming out of the womb telling my story ... then, I was going to put hands around the womb...hand prints touching... representing family ... trees growing from the womb because you have to make your own family ... but when I finished, I didn't like the way it turned out. It was like the same thing that happened to me. It didn't happen. I was stuck.

I wanted to make something else. I decided to change my art. I wasn't sure to what. I started drawing it on paper. I made a heart and wanted to put a poem on there. I decided to use that heart I made from before. I already made a heart out of paper towel, mod podge, and cloth. I thought this time the heart could symbolize another heart. That's their heart ... my kid's heart. I found some clip art online. It had adult hands and baby hands. The adult hands are holding the baby's hands. It was black and white. I colored the mother's hands my skin color and thought about what color my kid would be. There are hands on the heart now. That's supposed to be me as a mom someday and my kid. I want to show my baby so much love (see Figure 5.5).

Figure 5.5

My WIngs

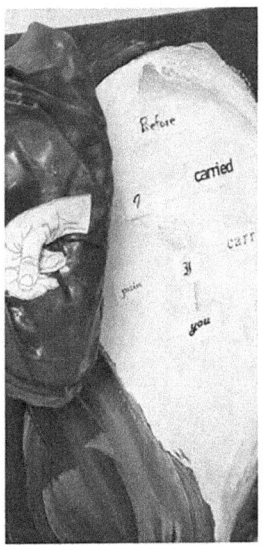

I decided at first to use a cork board. Then someone gave me a canvas. I never really painted before. I drew what I wanted to do. I wanted to put the heart in the middle and have angel wings on there. I also wanted to put a poem on there that I found. I was told about copyright and learned I can't say that's my work ... so I wrote my own poem ... I used my words. I was told that is more powerful to use my words. I see that now.

When everything dried, like the heart ... I wanted to paint now. I put the heart on a canvas. We used a hot glue gun and put it on there after I painted the wings. But first I wanted to make angel wings coming out from the heart. I wanted to find angel wings. I looked at some pictures of angel wings that were painted. I wanted to paint the wings. This was hard to do. I wanted to have a marble look to the wings. I tried many times to paint those wings. I was told it's just paint so I could keep painting until I liked it. I also learned you can't make mistakes in art. I didn't know that. It was a nice feeling to know there isn't a certain way to make the wings. It took time but I like the way it turned out now (see Figure 5.6).

Figure 5.6

My Artmaking

Those wings I painted are for my child because my child flies high. I made the wings white and pink. It took me a while to paint the wings ... like hours ... I never did this before, and I wanted it to turn out a certain way. I like the way they turned out.... The wings are like light colors like light energy colors. My child has love as energy.

I made the background black. The black because everything else didn't matter. I was just focused on one thing. I want to show that my baby will have all of my love. This will be my family someday. That's all I wanted to paint ... love.

I wrote my own poem and put it in different fonts to show that some points are bolder than other points. For example, I stressed the words "**I**," "**felt**,"and "**carried you**." I wrote this poem and mod podged it on the wings because these words lift my angel in the air:

> *Before I felt what true love*
> *Felt like you*
> *Before I carried pain I carried you*

This was a hard-ass journey. Doing the art, I was finally releasing this. It's all the art. I kinda feel better. I got to express myself. Sometimes it's hard to do this. It felt really good to let all of this out. Sometimes it is hard to talk about things and I just don't have the words ... but once I got started, I felt like I had something important to say. This art shows you love is the only thing that matters because it is the only thing we really need....and every child deserves to fly high and it's all because of love ... every child needs love...and I will give my child all the love ... all the love I have. I talked to people about this. I told them what this meant to me. This art ... it's a visual of how I feel, the art.

Advice

In school, I never did anything deep or based on me. I did other things I was assigned to do, but not having the freedom to make what I want or say what I want. Teachers and principals should be doing this work a lot more. They need to do this work on themselves. I think they should go through this too, so they understand what it's like. I think they should have something to say that is important to them. There are lots of things to talk about that are important.

Do art like this lets kids actually express themselves. If I would have had art in school, I don't know, maybe I would feel better ... in life ... in where I am at now ... but I think I would feel still feel shitty about things ... but I could get those shitty feelings out. There are so many kids going through shitty things, and they need a place to talk about this ... they need a place to express themselves...

Teachers and principals should learn about this. I don't think they learn this in school. If they did then they aren't doing it. I never saw this kind of art in my school. I think if teachers and principals don't know how to do this then they should learn this now. The sooner the better. There are a lot of kids out there that need to talk about what's on their mind. There are a lot of shitty things going on in the world. Every kid needs a family … and no one should ever be in the system … or not have a family … every kid needs to be loved … and if they don't have love … maybe they will do things that just aren't right…

I think teachers and principals should do this art themselves. Maybe do it with the students too. They need to experience it. They need to have a better understanding of what is happening throughout the process. They would also learn about themselves … and they could share what they learned with the kids too.

I think they should have to do it themselves. They need to think about what's going on in the world … what's important to them … what they experienced … what they did…. And after they do it, then they can teach, I guess. Maybe…. If they share with kids, then kids would see they can do this too and it's important to do. It shows it is not just kids … it's not just kids who have things on their mind or think about … it shows not to be afraid and learn deeper stuff about you. They know you actually care.

CHAPTER 6

HIRAETH

Quanae [Q]

The word "hiraeth" It's a Welsh word, a mixture between homesickness, nostalgia, and yearning ... yearning for something or an era of time that no longer exists. I wish I could go back to that time. I yearn for a time before colonization.... What would my life be like if my ancestors were not brought over from Africa? I think about this every day...I think about "What would my life had been?" In a tribe, peaceful, less traumatic? Wherever my family is from ... I have a longing to know. I yearn for a culture that is not coated in the blood, terror, and the suffering of my ancestors. This is my justice issue (see Figure 6.1).

Figure 6.1

My Painting With My Mom Standing Next to Me Holding My Hand

I want culture that has more depth than 400 years. I wish for a day of an era where hatred was not normalized. I want to go to school and learn about Black people and all of the contributions Black people have made. I never learned anything in school ... except about slavery. There is so much going on with Black people in this country. The real history and what is going on needs to be taught in school. It's not right. I learned everything from my mom. Where my mom was not affected by it ... all my family ... I've seen my family in poverty, dead, addicted, institutionalized. I'm not blaming it all on "the white man," I know we've been destroying ourselves too. We don't talk about this in school. We don't talk about what's really going on in this country and what needs to change. People need to know real history ... the truth (see Figure 6.2).

Figure 6.2

My Art Up Close

I guess I kind of started learning more about actual history. Probably like, when I became vegan two years ago. I started focusing more on spirituality and what's the bigger picture. When I realized how they processed meat and other animal products. I used to read about it. I don't even know what got me interested. I guess, my mom. She used to read a lot of Black history books. I learned from her. She would tell me if I asked her, but it was disturbing, so I didn't want to hear about it. Like, I remember I asked her about Emmit Till and when a whole bunch of Black people were lynched

Hiraeth 51

… they used her cancer cells for research and they wronged her … and if they can wrong her, who else can they wrong (see Figures 6.3 and 6.4).

Figure 6.3

People From the Public Discussing My Art

Figure 6.4

Gallery Owner and Local Vegan Chef (Who Made Food Aligned With Our Artmaking at Another Gallery Opening) Talking About the Exhibition

I didn't learn any of this in school. Because they want to cover up their guilt. A white child doesn't want to see what their parents or grandparents have done to us. That makes them uncomfortable. That's disturbing. I feel like it still needs to be taught. Otherwise, there are kids who are ignorant and then you have a lot of Black angry kids in the world. If you can see the real history instead of saying this never happened, people are going to riot and revolt. It's shown repeatedly in history, you cannot oppress people. People will find a way to revolt. They will revolt against whoever is oppressing them.

I don't feel like an old soul, but I have been told that. I have always been told that. I grew up around old people, so I love Shirley Temple, Popeye, Betty Boop, and trying to remember the other old cartoons. I was, what's the word, I was just ... I had a vast understanding of old movies ...

> *I love Black culture ...*
> *ever since I was a kid.*
> *But it was never taught in school.*
> *And that's why I kinda ...*
> *but that is why I also wanted to get away*
> *from Black culture*
> *because it is embedded in our culture ....*
> *You have bigger lips than me ...*
> *your skin is darker than me ...*
> *all this hate...*
> *hating on each other....*
> *We oppress the oppression and oppressing that oppression ...*
> *putting down ...*
> *down*
> *down ...*
> *who wants to be around that?*

I write poetry a lot. It is therapeutic. Probably like when I was in fifth grade when I was in like a lot of depression.

My Art

I wanted to paint a landscape of Africa. I wanted it to stand out. I wanted it to be about African culture. This is what is missing in school. I never saw people who looked like me. We didn't talk about Black culture in school. I decided to make this art about my roots.

It is a sunset. It's a copper sun. Sunsets have beautiful colors, and the colors represent hope to me. I don't know why, but they just do. Maybe it's because it's a journey and there is another day to see change.

I have been painting since I was drawing since whenever...it is therapeutic to me ... everything just washes away, and I know it will turn out good. I used art to relax ... to think ... to show what's on my mind.... That means the way I feel.

I painted an African sunset because of my roots. I put my mom and me on there. We are at the center because my mom is the center of my world. It's our silhouettes. I painted a fabric on us, and it is a certain fabric ... the type of design is called Kente. It's in our clothes. We are holding hands. That's my mom. There is so much love there. I learned everything about my roots ... the truth about what happens to Black people ... our culture ... history ... because of her. I would never have learned anything about this if it wasn't for me mom.

I felt peaceful and more connected and aligned with myself when I painted this. I became part of my painting in the process. I was in my own world.

I just want you to be awed ... to understand ... to empathize ... and maybe, just maybe you will feel inspired to do something about the real history ... maybe you will take time to learn about the real true history ... about what is happening in schools ... about the truth about Black culture ... maybe you will learn something new ... to learn something about my culture ... about my Black culture ... and learn something about yourself ... and then you can go out and share the truth ... and maybe you can inspire people to learn to ... and then maybe things will change in schools and I will see people like me and learn about the real history of Black people ... and all of the things we have done for this world ... for this country ... I don't think kids in school know unless they have a mom like my mom ... but I don't think they do ... and teachers and principals didn't seem to know anything either ... if they did then they aren't showing that to me or any other student.

Advice

I never did this work in school. I always did it on my own. That isn't right. They didn't let me do anything like this, not even in art class ... it was always boring ... like draw a little city ... it's always been boring ... this was different. I was told what to do in art class and never had the opportunity to think for myself until now. That's not right. Kids should be able to do this school. It doesn't matter what you are learning. It's a way to show what you learned and what something means to you. Sometimes we don't have words. We have to do it differently. Art lets me do that.

It was just very peaceful and felt one with myself ... very peaceful. School would have been so different for me if I was allowed to speak up and feel validated, I would have lived a different life. I felt alone in school. I didn't feel like I mattered. I didn't think anyone really cared about me or about my culture. It was like they were telling me I wasn't important ... but I know I am. I have been told I am an old soul. I think about things that maybe other kids don't think about. But you aren't going to know what kids think about if you don't give them an opportunity to learn...and to think. I don't think I would have been in residential treatment if I had art in school... like this art. I had a lot of anger inside. I didn't have a way to let it out. I didn't have anyone to talk to. The teachers and principal didn't know about me. They didn't ask about me. I am pretty quiet. I don't trust a lot of people. I don't it past somebody. I needed a space to express myself in art. That didn't happen in school. It should. It should happen for all kids. We need it.

Art should be there at any age for kids. That might be a great coping skill. That could save the life of a kid, especially if they don't have anything. This should not have been the first time I was allowed to talk about my culture or what's on my mind.

Teachers and principals should be aware of all kids and very educated about real history ... and not to be insensitive to people's problems.... It should be required for teachers and principals to love all of their kids ... like, why would you not? They should also be giving kids art to do so they can express themselves too. Art saved me. Did you hear that? It saved me.

Teachers need to be sensitive ... aware of what real history is ... and be trauma aware. There are actually laws about telling teachers they need to help us with learning about our emotions. It is so wrong when they don't. And then there are laws trying to get passed that stop teachers and students from learning about all of this! Learning about my culture? Who is trying to pass these laws? They need to know to get past the uncomfortableness. We will never be able to advance as a society. It is not about forgiving and forgetting. We need to start another era. This is so wrong and so weird. No one ever told me about this until now. Why did I have to wait until now to know? I feel like I can't do much about it. I am in here. What will you do?

I am giving the money I made from my art to the Karamu Performing Arts Theater if my art sells. I had a lot of people tell me they wanted it and then they would give the money to them. I want my culture to be shared ... to be valued.

CHAPTER 7

FAMILY LOVE

J

I want to do art on girls' and boys' rights. Because of the abuse and domestic abuse and attempted murder. I want to focus on these rights because this happened to me. I want my art to focus on me. No kid should ever have to be abused or see people in their family get hurt or attempted murder. All kids should have families that love each other ... don't hurt each other ... all kids need love ... and that's what I want for every kid ... every family ... that's all (see Figure 7.1).

Figure 7.1

My Imaginary Parents in My Art

56 J

Once upon a time I was a runaway…

So … I was on the run by myself for a long time. I want people not to make the mistakes I made because I kept going back to him … he threw me on the ground and bashed my head into the wall … he dragged me … he threw me down … he ripped out some of my hair … he left marks on me … he damn near killed me …I am trying to think what else … he threatened me … he wouldn't let me and my friend leave up out of the house … he held us in the house for two hours … the only reason he wouldn't let us leave is because he knew I would have called the police on him … it was like some weeks later I called the police … they went to his house and he wasn't there … nothing happened to him … he did aggressive and abusive stuff to me … he shot at me multiple times … he got up in my friend's face and yelled at her … we were in a boyfriend/girlfriend relationship, but I cut him off the day I came here. I have been here a month (see Figures 7.2 and 7.3).

Figure 7.2

Mother Holding Children

Figure 7.3

A Sister and Brother

Another guy didn't do that much ... he threw me into a wall and threw me onto the ground ... that's it ... it was a long story ... I remember it like it was yesterday ... I tell them the story and I don't skip no parts ... I want to tell that story over and over again ... he was 18 and I was 14 ... he 19 now ... the bottom line is that I don't want people to make the mistakes I made ... he grown ... and I'm not. I want to tell the full story now. This one day, I picked up my best friend and then I had my other friend in the car with me already ... and then, that's when we had made plans ... she was in the car with me ... she went to her boyfriend's house ... my best friend had nowhere to go because her family disowned her so I took her with me to my boyfriend's house. We spent one night there. We smoked with him that night. There were four of us, including him and his sister. After that, the next day came. We were eating breakfast, and he rolled some weed. There was no food in the refrigerator. He said he would go to the store with his homeboy and get some breakfast food. And I said, okay. And then after that, I went upstairs with his sister. And then, my other, my best friend, she stayed downstairs. And me and his sister was just talking, and that's when I seen him come back and then after that, he was looking for his weed he rolled and put on the table ... and then he came back and asked me where his weed was...me and his sister told him we don't know ... and that's when I told him to ask the girl ... and he went down there and asked her ... she said she don't know ... that's when he called me and his sister down there ... we had come downstairs ... he asked us again where his weed was

… and to ask my best friend because she was the only one down there … that's when he got mad … and that's when my best friend said she wanted to go … I already knew something was up … and then that's when she said she wants to go … he said ain't nobody going anywhere until I get my weed back … I went to give him my bags … my bookbag and duffle bag and my little red purse … he checked them and wasn't nothing in there … that's when my best friend gave him her bags … he checked them and there wasn't nothing in there … he checked her purse and it was in there … that's when he looked at me and said he should beat me for letting my friend steal his weed … he kicked her out … she went downstairs and I told her not to touch nothing … that's when he slammed the door and locked it … that's when he told his sister to go upstairs … he came to me and said he should beat my ass…he threw me into the ground … threw me into the wall … he bashed my head in … shot at me … I called one of my hommies to come and get us … he came and picked us up … I dropped her off and then I went to my other homeboy house … I still got the marks on me to this day … I don't wear shorts … or I wear a hoodie or a long sleeve shirt … I cut him off … and I have been here a month … I did a trial to live with my family … I have been in foster care two times … I am not here to make friends. I am focusing on me, and I want to get up out of here … I help people out … I work outside of here … I work in an office, and I work with kids, they toddlers … I need to play catch up with all of my work … because at my job, I am a staff and a supervisor. I like doing both … I got school and work to do … I have to pay a lot of stuff when I get out of here (see Figures 7.4 and 7.5).

I feel like when the teenager males hit a female, they don't get in trouble for it. The police don't do nothing to nobody nowadays. But when a female hits a male, they go to jail or get in trouble. I feel that's unfair.

Art

I don't think I am an artist. I said that. I smiled when I made my painting. I never painted before. I had lots of nice things said to me. Everybody loved my painting. They couldn't believe I did this. I did. I painted their skin colors. Everyone had a different brown … different hair … I wanted the girls to have things in their hair (see Figure 7.6).

I wanted to do a painting on children's rights. Everyone should have a family who loves them. I made a painting of a family. This is a Black family. There is a father, mother, two sisters, and two brothers. This is the family I think every kid should have. In this family, everybody loves each other. Everybody is nice to each other. The father is putting his arms around the

Family Love 59

Figure 7.4

Siblings

Figure 7.5

A Woman Looking at My Art and Reading About It

Figure 7.6

Using Fabric and Paint

mother. The mother is putting her arms around the two girls and the two boys. The boys and girls love each other. They feel that (see Figure 7.7).

I used fabric for the clothes. I wanted it to be soft. I used mod podge and fabric. I picked out what I wanted. I painted black on the outside of every person…and then I put fabric on the inside. I cut pieces of fabric with scissors. I put mod podge on there and then I put the fabric down and then I mod podged over it. Then I used a hairdryer to make it dry faster. When it was dry, I painted black around it again. I really like the fabric. This is what love is … it's soft. The father, mother, girls, and boys are happy and feel loved (see Figure 7.8).

Every child deserves this. I wrote this …

I want this for me.
For my future.

Advice

I didn't like school. I didn't go to school. I needed love. They need to love me. I feel loved here. I feel like they care about me. It just feels different. I never did this before. It felt good to have people say nice things about me … and they asked about the painting. I got to tell them what it was about. Schools have to teach kids. They don't have to love them …

Family Love 61

Figure 7.7

Using Fabric to Symbolize Softness and Warmth

Figure 7.8

Every Child Deserves a Loving Family

they just have to teach … they ain't their kids … I feel like teachers love me here … this ain't something I had before … teachers just did their job … that's why they teach…. They don't have to love them, they ain't their kids. You mean to kids, then you hurt them. I don't want that. It is just different here in school.

CHAPTER 8

DARKNESS FALLING

Kano

My art is about protecting my mom. I didn't like how she was treated. I wanted it to stop. I couldn't help her or stop it. I wish I had powers. I like the Joker. I used to like him, but now I like Lobo. He killed Santa Clause. He has an awesome chain weapon and a dog and a really cool bike. He kills for fun. He just kills. He is crazy. He came out of his stomach killing. He killed his parents … he killed his doctor … and everyone on his planet … I don't what his planet is called or where it is in comic books … I have seen it on Death Battles … they just grab a bunch of random people and fight to the death. I don't know how to read actually. I just learn from Mike. He is Mom's friend. He teaches me things. He teaches me to respect my mother (see Figure 8.1).

Figure 8.1

I Wanted to be the Protector

He used to teach me about comic books, but not anymore. I don't know why. I never talk about him anymore. I don't talk about comic books anymore. This is acid from the Joker's flowers. If I am not corrected, I think it burns your face off, but I don't know. I used to watch Ash v. Evil Dead, but I don't anymore because Melissa moved far away. She was a babysitter. I still see Mike at my house. But he is not supposed to be there because he beat Mom in the face. I have been through a lot. He will probably still be there. No contact order. The police did it. I am afraid he is going to be there. I can't remember when I talked with her (see Figure 8.2).

Figure 8.2

A Cast of My Body

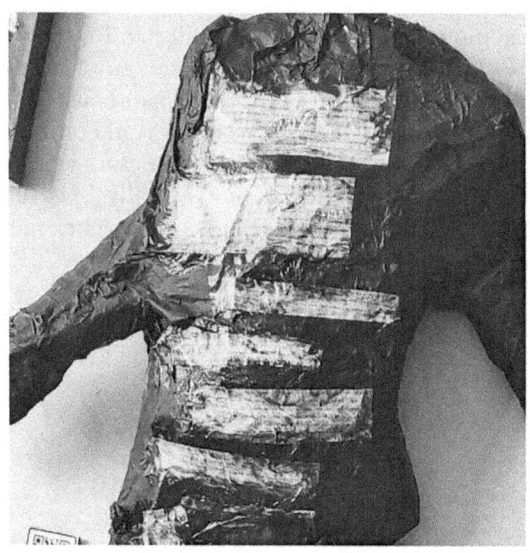

I wish I had powers like Lobo because he is invincible. He never gets hurt and he never dies. And the Joker, well, he never dies. I would probably be punching Mike for hurting my Mom, but that would hurt, but it wouldn't hurt. It hurts because I saw my Mom get hurt. I think she was punched, but I can barely remember… pushed her into the window… and smashed in the back of the head. And he says, "Oh, I thought you were a White guy covered in tatoos …" and then apparently that "White guy" beat his mother, so he thought he "envisioned" the guy who beat his mother. He thought it was him, but it was her. I don't believe it. How could he think that wasn't my Mom. And that hurt me … to see him beat my Mom and lie (see Figure 8.3).

Figure 8.3

My Art in an Art Gallery

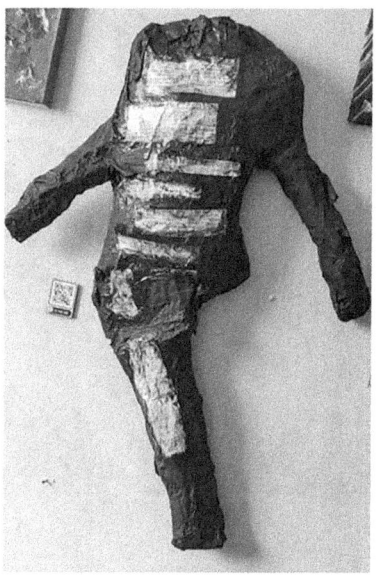

I would not be hurt by Mike because I would have power … I would hurt him … for hurting me and my mom … and he pushed me into the wall … he told my Mom I was lying … I wasn't lying … and sadly she still believes that pain in the butthead today … and there was another guy before being pushed … Bam Bam hit me in the head with a baseball bat … I was living with my mom … I lived with her until I came here (see Figure 8.4).

I just love villians. Villians are … creepy … I do like creepy … I watch kill counts … Dead Meat is a YouTuber … he counts kills in horror movies…and that's how I watch my horror movies … it was a new movie on the channel … Forever Purge … and then before I came here, I said, oh, it's on there … they copied some kills from another movie … they have the Purge … a lot of Purge movies … the Forever Purge…just a bunch of Purge movies … when I grow up I will be an ice cream man … and sadly to say, I am going to come back for them … all the bullies … all the bullies who ever bullied me … you want to bully me, I am going to do what I want to do to you … I am going to be like Rod … he was bullied for being chubby … and then he became the killer ice cream man … he made special ice cream to get kids fat … I am not going to do that … I am going to … well, it might never happen … because I don't like that much gore … I kept dreaming about it … I might have a gun on me, but that's about it … that's for protection (see Figure 8.5).

Figure 8.4

A Man Came and Said This was a Powerful and Moving Exhibition

Figure 8.5

A Teacher Read and Looked at My Art and was Moved

Darkness Falling 67

This song gives me memories of my Mom ... Tik Tok ... my Mom is not dead [listening to Scrubs]...

Kids have bullied me ... like Keegan ... he is not here ... he is fat and ugly ... he called me names and kicked me and flipped me off ... I hit him in the head two times because he ripped up something Angel drew. He is my friend. I was upset. It was Sunrise and Moondrop from Security Breech, that's a video game. I was defending my friend and my papers too. He was not happy. Trust me, Angely was not happy (see Figure 8.6).

Figure 8.6

The Public Viewing My Artmaking

All of my toys got thrown away at Melissa's. My mom told me to get one toy at a time, but I couldn't. I didn't get all of my army soldiers ... and flippin cheeses ... ImagineX ... and also TreasureX ... if you get the sets ... I lost only ImagineX ... and I was mad one day and broke my action Joker figure. I was mad, but I don't know ... Mike gave it to me to calm down, but it didn't work. I broke it and threw it. I am very sad about that ... I told myself, "Straighten out, you dummy." He was important to me. My second-grade teacher bought me that. I couldn't repair him. Even if I could, my Mom said I had to throw it out. I wanted to keep the head at least, but my Mom said no. I wanted to keep the head for memories because my teacher gave that to me (see Figure 8.7).

Figure 8.7

My Art in Another Exhibition

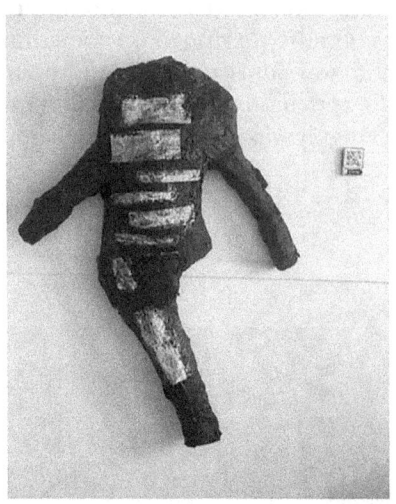

I never wrote a poem. This is my first poem:
I want to protect people.
I love my Mom …
I love my friends …
Angel, Drake, Dominic, and MacKenzie,
and one more, Armis,
but he is now friends with Keegan.
I want all the powers in the world.
I want to be a genie.
If only I had a bunch of wishes …
I would wish I had all the powers in the world
and I wish I was a genie.
Well, I would serve masters
and I would be happy,
a little bit.
I might say, "I am not making you eggs …"
I would tell them to learn how to make their own eggs.
I want to give them wishes about love.
That's important,
not eggs …
You want this fancy stuff?
Do it on your own.
Why?
Because love is more important.
It's what I want
and what people need (see **Figure 8.8**).

Darkness Falling 69

Figure 8.8

Hiding My Poem on My Body

I like rap rock. I bet all of this will change when I grow up. Maybe I will find better stuff. YouTubers like Mark Applier, Think Noodles, and FGTV (fun, I guess) … Dac Blake … and Kindly Keon and I think that's about it … and then there is some guy who breaks into games and tells the secrets (see Figure 8.9).

Figure 8.9

Mod Podge My Story Because It is Part of Me

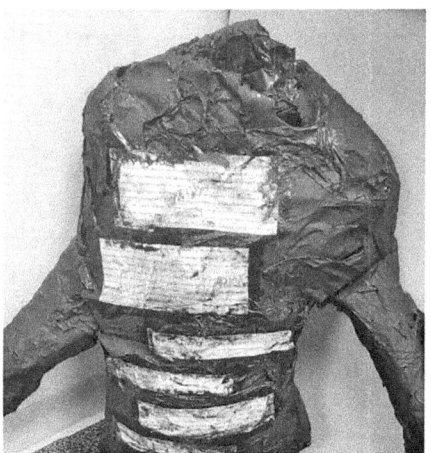

I have so much to say .... my art will say something important. You need to know that.

My Art

I decided to make myself. I wanted to be like Noob. I made my body out of tape, black garbage bags, paper towel, paint, and mod podge. I had to get taped up. I had a garbage bag around my ches t... and then my leg. When I was taped up, it felt weird. I felt like a mummy. I wasn't sure what was going to happen. After I was taped up, it felt all right. I saw my body in tape and said, "Wow! That's me!" I was excited. I never did this before. I wanted to do this for Halloween. It was cool.

I painted my body black. I wanted it black. I wanted to make it Noob. He is a character from Mortal Combat. He has a shadow blackish gooey stuff ... it's like his shadow and fights with him. That's why it's black. His fatality is great. You might not like it because it's gory.

I put my story of my life on my chest. This is the story you are reading. I also put my poem on there. I covered my body with it. It's about me. I wanted the black on there. It makes it like kinda cool ... like it's hidden. That is like what I do. I am private. I don't tell everyone my story.

I think other kids want powers too. They might want to protect their mom.

I think it looks great! I really like this. It turned out better than I thought it would. I actually didn't know how it would turn out ... I wanted to put a head on it...with a mask and have two legs kicking out to push people away ... to kick ... but I like the way it turned out. I think it looks good without the head ... and just one leg ... it's kinda like I couldn't kick back ... but I wish I had powers.

I would do this again. I liked it. I like doing this. I never did anything like this before. Other kids should try this ... even the teachers ... I wonder what they would do for this ... I thought about that.

Advice

I think all kids should be doing this work and remember to be there for the kids. Don't let them do this alone. Adults might not know how to help another kid and they need help. I talked and I don't do that. It is hard for me to trust. I learned I can talk, and people care. I said what I needed to say. I did what I wanted to do. I think kids should be doing this art, but you need to be older, not a really little kid. They need a lot of help. They need someone to talk to ... they need someone to help them. Kids really need this. I hope they do this in school.

CHAPTER 9

ALL EQUAL

Nitro

I am doing my art on racism and White supremacy. This is my justice issue. I see this happening a lot and it is not something I like to watch. I get mad at three things: (1) if you touch my family; (2) if you touch me; and (3) if you are a racist. Family matters to me and I never had a family. I am adopted. It's different. I basically taught yourself everything growing up … how to walk…how to eat … how to use the restroom … I have been in foster care for eight years … I just got adopted a year ago … I probably moved from eight or nine houses … it was hard to want to stick around and I finally found the right person so I can let them do their thing … it took six months to get started … it took about six and a half more months to go to court and then it was finished. I consider my family my dad, my two brothers, and basically my grandparents. Most of my birth family is not here anymore and I haven't talked to them in at least five years. I call him Anthony (see Figure 9.1).

72 NITRO

Figure 9.1

Up Close Photo and Paint Streak

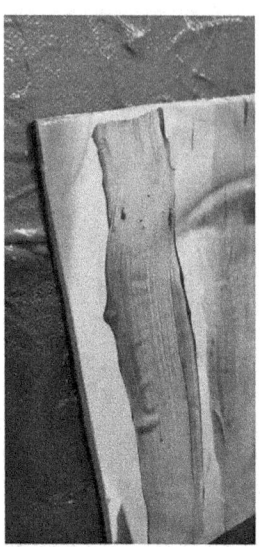

I have two brothers XXX and XXX. I don't really like Noah as much as Matthew because he is taller than me. My grandparents are pretty chill. My grandpa is usually hunting or doing something on his own. If they actually hurt them, it depends on what it was, but I wouldn't want to get in trouble for it. It's a tough situation. I hope nothing really happens. I am a human too. We bleed the same blood. If you are going to hurt them where it's traumatizing. You can't just beat someone because you feel like it. I know um that most people are like chill and cool but there is always that one person. I fight back because I am not going to let them just hurt me. For a good example, someone yelled the "n" word at a staff. I almost fought him because of it. It is just wrong. There are so many other words you can use to get your point across (see Figure 9.2).

I learned this by myself. I lived in the ghetto. I was called a cracker all the time. I have never been at a "normal" school. It pushed me to become better. And now, I am a quarterback. I broke my collarbone. I was the secondary quarterback and had 79 touchdowns, and you have 3 to 5 seconds to think fast or else they are going to throw you down. I am not even left-handed, but it hurts to throw that fast and far. Once it gets better, I am going to work out and stuff. I do 20 pushups before lunch and after ... and 20 before and after dinner (see Figures 9.3 and 9.4).

A normal school will have some bullies, but the school I went to the students had guns in school. You could smoke and you wouldn't get in

All Equal 73

Figure 9.2

Getting Closer to Understanding Me

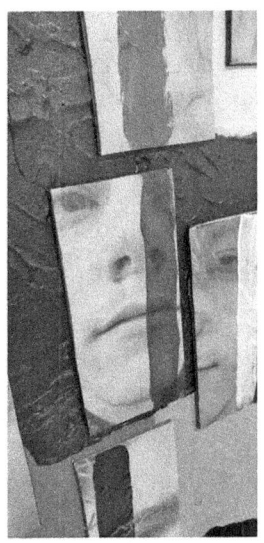

Figures 9.3 and 9.4

Discovering Myself and My Part in All of This

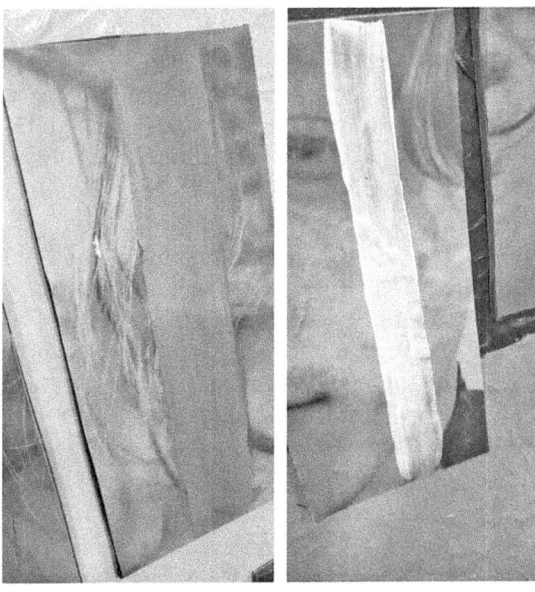

trouble. It was in Meadowdale. It's a couple hours away. I learned about racism there. Well, obviously, since it was 99% like African American people, no one was nice to anybody. They would use the "n" word and I asked one time, and I almost had the shit beat out of me. It's not something anyone taught me. I had to learn this by myself.

My dad was a racist person. He overdosed. He abused me my entire life. He put gallons of soap down my face and almost beat me to death and sexually, emotionally, neglect me, and physically abuse me. He wasn't a good person. My mom didn't do anything about it. She would laugh and do something like that. And during her beatings, there was nothing I could do about it. I was like 6 or 7. My mom shot herself. I saw her. She had it on a recording. I was the person who found it on the floor. We were going to the house…me, my uncle, and my sister … we just got out of foster care for two weeks … we found her dead and the phone and that's what happened … there was nothing wrong with her in my opinion … I had not seen her for a few years … she did drugs as well … that's a lot of trauma … I laugh it now …I t is like a coping mechanism … I try not to think about it because it is not worth thinking about…I did talk about it a while ago … some people think it is isolating … I just do video games … I wonder what the world would be like if people used technology to cope … I have been in several fights … like a guy hitting a girl … I get in fights … I can't get over that … you can't just hit a girl … I don't see a purpose in hitting a girl who is under 16 or 5' 5". I have never hit a girl and I am pretty happy about that. I don't care if a girl hits me. I have taken beatings a ton of times, so it doesn't really hurt anymore. Power and abusing that power is different. It's how you use your power that matters. Mr. Morris taught me a little bit about this. I learned about Hitler. I just learned he was White. That surprises me. I thought he would be Jewish or something and he wanted to take over to be in power or something. I want to learn more about it.

White people like taking over the world and yeah … and all the wealth. I learned about this growing up in the world. How not a lot of minorities don't have opportunities and everyone in the world can share and bring people together. Honestly, I don't know why White people think they can do that. The government is corrupt. They don't give equal opportunities to every citizen like jobs and money. They like to take over businesses and not leave room for other people. I am White. I haven't really grown up around White people. I grew up and saw how other people were treated. I saw the other side. I wouldn't say all White people are bad, but things need to be fixed. Black people and Mexicans are being shot down with opportunities for jobs. A White person can go interview for a job and then a Black person, but they just pick the White person. I want my art to make a difference. I am not really a social person, and I don't really present things to people, but I want to bring awareness. People will see that they need to be fair to everyone all around. Not everybody … not one certain race needs to dominate. We need to work together to make that happen. How people view other people and who they want to hang out with and why. You have the separation of Black and White people. It's about changing their viewpoint.

    I learned about systemic racism. This means it's your perception about race and it's through environmental factors like peers, school, family, teachers, what society thinks is okay, and laws. Laws and rules tell us who we can go to school with…. Racism is still in today's society. I thought it was different, but it's not. This just happened in Mississippi. They had a segregated school before 2019. White parents were fighting for their White students to attend White schools and Black students to attend Black schools (see https://www.clarionledger.com/story/news/local/2019/04/02/segregation-mississippi-classrooms-parental-request-policy-elementary-brookhaven/3291509002/). It was surprising to me. I thought all of this was past us. Another example is prom in Georgia in 2014 (see https://www.cnn.com/2014/04/04/living/integrated-prom-wilcox-county-georgia/index.html). They just allowed Black and White students to go to prom together. This doesn't surprise me. We, White people, segregate ourselves because of fear. We are afraid of what we don't know and when we don't know. Then, when we don't know, this makes us view people as negative. We need to be aware of our perceptions and be open to change and culturally working together. Systemic racism is made up of how society takes care of the people and supports the people in different ways such as healthcare options, salaries, jobs, where you go to school, how much money you make, and treated differently by the government and law enforcement all because of their skin color (see https://www.raceforward.org/videos/systemic-racism).

    I learned that the Europeans came over and they owned land. They didn't want to work, so they tricked their servants to coming over and they worked for free. They had other Europeans called indentured servants and Africans who were also indentured servants. Then the people with money told the European indentured servants, you are free. We will give you land, and you can patrol the African indentured servants. This was power. The Europeans who had land thought they were better than the African indentured servants that worked for them for free and had no freedom.

    The slave owners looked at their slaves as property. They just wanted to maintain their money and income. And then, the Civil War happened because the South didn't want to pay taxes on their "so-called property." I think that is really inhumane. Every human is human, and we are all the same. People back then viewed other people as different or below them.

    The poor White people were told to fight for the South. They wanted the poor White people to think they were better than the slaves, but they didn't have slaves. They were poor too. The White people who were slave owners would not hire a poor White person because they would have to pay them. They are going to keep slaves because they work for free. The White people who were slave owners had to think of a way to trick the poor White people to fight for them.

When people from Mexico, like immigrants, come to the United States, White people fear that because they are told "they" are taking their jobs and "money." And then, White people fear them because they think they are losing something, but they are not. They are gaining a lot because they get a lot more stuff done, and we do not pay them the money they deserve. They come here and do low-paying jobs. And then, the rich people make the profit. But White people fear the immigrants, which keeps people segregated, and that causes racism. Like I said, it's a system.

White people are believing this stuff. When the poor Whites in New Orleans had a hurricane, they lost homes and their money. So did the poor Black people who lived so many yards away. The poor White people blamed the Black people for the flooding. They even tried to change or go around the law to make sure only blood relatives could go back and rent or buy property. This really meant that White people wanted the Blacks out, but they couldn't say that, so they made up this law. They lost in court, but what they should have done was to think about the government not caring about all of the poor people who were Black and White. You gotta put the idea in someone's head that "they are not good" or they would not benefit from being with Black people. You gotta keep us separate, which is a lie. We should be working together. Rich White people don't want that because they want to dominate.

Art

It was fun to do this. I think it turned out pretty good. Just doing this with a group of people and what this is all about. I never painted before. I am 16 almost 17 years old. Every year we talk about racism and talk about Hitler and say he was racist, but that's it. It's just about that, not about racism here or what is really happening with police brutality or putting Black people in jail (see Figure 9.5).

I chose colors because each one shows a different race or group of people. We are all really connected. We took pictures of different parts of my face. I asked my teacher to print them. She printed them in black and white.

I did my face to show there are different parts of me. I am not just White. There are different parts of me. When we see Black people, White people just look at the color of someone. They don't see the different parts. I blew up different parts and put them on all of the colors. I used hot glue to do this. I mod podge the pictures on foam core. I put the colors on the pictures because this is to show that we are really equal. We are not treated that way.

Figure 9.5

Putting My Ideas Together

I am in different shapes and colors to show that we are really together, but we just look different.

We need to be treated with respect. There shouldn't be different treatment for different people. We are connected (see Figure 9.6).

I used foam core and made the photos of my face stand out. This was to show I am part of something. I stand out just like this should stand out. People should care about this stuff.

It had a good back story. The whole thing is about racism and what we need to do. I never did anything like this before. I would definitely do this again.

Advice

I think we need to have more broad views in school. You only hear huge topics like Hitler and KKK or slavery, but we don't learn about what is really going on … still … l ike you can teach this … why aren't they? I never knew about racism or police brutality or about how many Black people are in jail or about how hate still happens.

Figure 9.6

My Art in a Public Art Space

I think teachers and principals should learn this from their bosses. They should look at this and their past. Was this a big issue when they were in school? Have things really changed? If they don't know this stuff, we have electronics, and they should be looking this stuff up and learn from the internet. It's on them if they don't want to learn. College is what they should be learning … it should be taught in high school … you should learn about racism in school … they might need to be taking classes like this about racism and police brutality and what is really going on in the world if they want to be teachers or principals … they need to know this so they can teach their students … it would be better for them if they did.

I think teachers and principals should be tested on this. If they are racist or don't want to learn about this stuff, they should not be teaching … that's my opinion. The college should be giving them a test to find out if they are ready to really work with all students and know this stuff. If they don't pass, then they don't teach.

I never did anything like this in school. I didn't know anything about the real history of what's going on with Black people and how White people have treated Black people. I just learned all of this. The only thing I knew was there was racism, but I didn't understand why.

I asked if my art sold to donate the money to the Diversity Center. I researched them and found out they work with people to help them understand why this is important ... everything I wrote about and did my art on.

We should have this in school. I never did something like this where I learned about this. I wanted to know more about this. I did some research and learned a lot of things I didn't know. I learned about me. I learned that what I think is important too. I learned that I do make a difference and used my art to say things I never said before. Then I decided to make my art about what I learned. Every student should have the chance to do this. I don't know why schools don't do this. They should.

CHAPTER 10

ALEXITHYMIA

T1

I want to focus on my life for my art. I have been through a lot. My story ... I read a story #MeToo ... and they share their traumas and experiences. That kind of helped me see that those things happened to other people. I don't have to be stuck in the past. It helped me. I can move forward. I would say about two weeks ago, my friend went to the library and gave me this to read. It was different people sharing their stories. It inspired me to share mine. They were able to share their stories and I want to publish this and help other people because it had an impact on me (see Figure 10.1).

Figure 10.1

Working on the Details

My trauma started when I was five. My older brother's friend would come over and put his hand in my private areas. He stuck his hand in my pants and they were inside of me. I was in my room with my mom, and I didn't want her to change me. I told her what happened. The cops were called and stuff. The cops called his mother, and she told them this was not the first time this happened (see Figure 10.2).

Figure 10.2

My Art is in a Gallery for the Second Time

I don't know what he looks like anymore. Whenever my family goes to this festival, they see him, but I don't. We leave if they see him. Nothing happened to him. He wasn't arrested or taken to court or anything. To be honest, I don't know why. He is not the only person who has done this to me. It happened again with my friend's dad. He massaged me (see Figure 10.3).

My mom was always working third shift. My brother was always out. I would take care of my siblings and stuff around the house. He was also my mom and brother's drug dealer. They probably didn't think he was suspicious. Nothing happened. The cops were called. Nothing was done about him (see Figure 10.4).

My family told me to stay away. I told the cops everything. They said okay, but there wasn't evidence. At 14, I ran away because I didn't want to go back into the system. I was staying with my mom without anyone knowing. I had a party without anyone knowing. I was trying to get shit faced. I was on the floor with this guy. I told him I was drunk, and he stopped. The

Alexithymia 83

Figure 10.3

Screaming

Figure 10.4

People from the Community at My First Art Exhibition

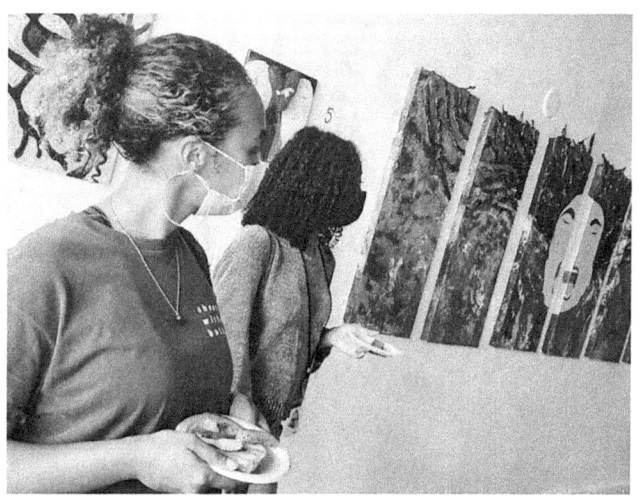

dude I was laying with, and this other guy came over. He was my friend. He put his arm by my leg. I told the dude to stop but he said it wasn't him. I told my friend to stop, but he didn't stop. I called someone and asked them to come as soon as possible. I was a runaway, and I was afraid. I thought this person was my friend, and I didn't want to get him in trouble. From there, I left. I told my older brother, and he threatened him and told him to go back to where he lived. I hung out with a guy friend for a couple of days and then with my ex. He was with someone else, but I didn't want anything sexually with him. He would kiss up on me. He kept trying and trying, and I told him no. I thought it would escalate from there. He would tell me it was okay, but it wasn't. I stayed with my girlfriend from there and things go better. I kinda just felt alone in the situation. I couldn't turn to anyone. I couldn't tell me mom because she wasn't in the picture. That's who I talked to … I felt like I was in the middle of the icy water on a piece of ice … I was surrounded by the hungry whales … I felt like an otter and I fell in the water because I was trying to escape all the things around me … I feel like once I was in the water … I was fighting … but I wanted to give up … all these things pushing me down … I just wanted to come back up and get into a safe zone. For an otter, it would be a flat surface of ice to wait out everything. And in real life, I need to be surrounded by positive people who want me to achieve these things that I want and need to accomplish instead of the whales trying to kill me or bring me down or drown me and take my life (see Figure 10.5).

Figure 10.5

The Panels Together

Alexithymia 85

This is a poem I wrote for my art. I am proud of it. And I made certain words like "Relief" and "Courage" big and bold because those are the words I want you to pay attention to. It's how I am feeling when I do this art. It's what I am trying to tell you. Here it is …

I am not one to open up a lot.
But I shore did.
Relief.
Weight off my shoulders.
For a very long time,
I didn't tell anyone my story.
I felt weak.
But when I shared,
it took a lot off of my shoulders.
Courage.
I didn't know I had it in me.
It feels great
because I opened up
I opened up to somebody new.
That's It (see Figure 10.6).

Figure 10.6

A Man Reading About My Art and Said This was Amazing

My Art

I want to use six canvases to symbolize the true feelings I have inside because I don't have the words. Sometimes I don't feel whole. I feel fragmented, but after doing I don't feel connected to myself, so I have several canvases, but they are connected with me drowning in the water. I put myself in the middle of my art because this is about my story. I want you to learn from my life story. I don't want anyone to feel alone (see Figures 10.7 and 10.8).

Figure 10.7

My Eyes

The mouth Is open Ie I am screaming because I am scared. I am crying out for help. I am under the water. It is hard to understand what I am saying. No one can hear. That is how I felt in my life. It felt like while I was speaking and being open and honest about what was going on, no one really heard me. They heard the words, but they weren't listening (Figures 10.9).

My eyes are closed because I don't to see the negative things in my life. I am afraid to see what is ahead of me and what the future holds. I think I might just see reality once my eyes are open. At some point in my life, I want to be able to open my eyes. I feel like the key to opening my eyes is being able to accept people in … and to be loved … and to be cared for …

Figure 10.8

I am Working on My Art

Figure 10.9

Closer Look at the Hair

my cheeks are pink because that is typically what I see for Valentine's Day ... pink and red ... I want to come above the water and surface.

I need to feel loved first by family and those who I have grown up with and who I classify as family before I can go to the surface ... I was told blood doesn't make you family ... it makes you related ... my friends are like siblings ...

I have my hair going up because I am sinking ... it goes into the other sections because it's still me ... I am in the deep ... there are parts of me trying to go to the surface ... the other parts are struggling ... many people would float to the surface ... but not me ... not right now ...I t's like pressure is being put on me ... I feel like the pressure comes with words ... not someone holding me other ... it's the negative that people say to me that keeps coming into existence ... it's the negative words and thoughts that keep holding me under ... I am drowning (Figures 10.10)

Figure 10.10

My Hair

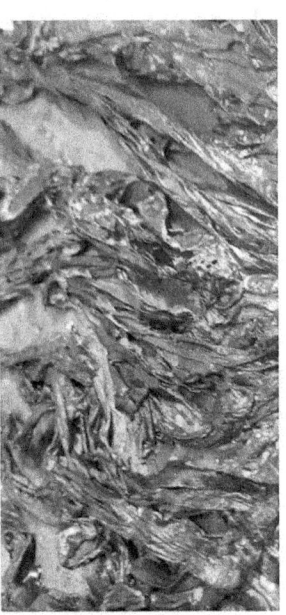

I have kind of began to understand my self-worth and to become confident in myself ... I am learning not to dwell on this ... I want to be a better me and inspire people...and help people who have shared similar feelings I have felt ... I want to help them ... to know they are not alone ... when I reach the surface ... I will be a better person than before ... I will be a new and improved me ... right now, it feels like it is miles away from the surface ... but in reality it is only inches ... I can see the surface ... it gives me motivation and strength to want to reach the top ... that's about it ... for so long I was waiting for a hand to reach down and pull me up for air ... but I only have myself and it takes my own self to pull me up from underneath. (Figures 10.11)

Figure 10.11

Drowning

I haven't done anything like this before. I feel inspired and hopeful for my future. This art and telling my story is the next step in my life and it is helping me to do this. I feel like a lot of the colors express my emotions. Instead of bottling them up inside, it's a way to share it and express it and to share what I am really feeling inside.

> *Dear to the People Reading This:*
>
> *Growing up, I felt like my voice was never being heard. Therapists would sit across from me and listen to what I had to say, but never really understood me or even heard what I had to say. Teachers, family, friends, and even my own mother and father. On the inside I was drowning in ALEXITHYMIA, a feeling of not knowing how to explain they way you feel. Deep sorrow, sadness or depression, grief, intense distress always running through my mind ... never truly had time to grow within myself because I was dwelling on the past why nobody heard what I was feeling. I was stuck. Over time, I learned how to express my emotions and feelings through art. Not just drawing and coloring, but painting and storytelling ... even writing poems ... that is where true art lies in my opinion ... going at every project with 110% effort and being true to yourself and about the meaning behind the project. In school, my art teacher would teach us to shade and make sure we got the shapes just right, but they never really told us to put our feelings into our piece. A feeling that makes our pieces unique. Teachers criticized us and told us our work was not good enough or we did something the wrong way, but in reality, the piece is amazing just the way it is.*

Once the art was done, I felt relieved. The way I was feeling just fine and got out. I didn't have to lie to myself anymore. It was just out. At first, I just wanted a little canvas. I felt so small in this big world. I learned I am not small using six canvases. I am here. You can see me. I am overcoming these feelings.

Advice

To the teachers and principals of schools all over the world: I feel you should be teaching kids the importance of expressing their feelings, whether that be through art or writing assignment. Art isn't just an extra curriculum, but a way to acknowledge their feelings and personalities. While doing this art, I thought I wouldn't be able to get the tools that I needed to complete my ideas because growing up, people would tell me that they would do and/or buy something for me, but never followed through with it. I began to realize nobody has your back 100% like you do. You can't depend on other people for your happiness.

Teachers and principals can't be trained to do this. They just tell us how to do the assignment and how to do it. But that is not what we did here. We used our creative minds and were allowed to be creative and express ourselves. This is not something that people can just be trained in. I feel like everything is at free will. It would be healthy for teachers and principals to grow with their minds and do things outside of their comfort zones to explain what you are experiencing and what you are doing (Figures 10.12).

Figure 10.12

My Art Eith Other Artmaking From Youth

I think growing is about expressing themselves in a positive manner. I didn't have that in schools. I didn't have that in my household either. I think school is a time and a place for a break from the stressors, the things going on in our lives. This is a way to work through and talk about things on our minds, what we are going through, someone's trauma, and understanding how to express yourself.

I feel like while I was painting, I was painting a girl that was me … and by doing this … I reflected on my 16 years of life and how I have grown so much … and all I had accomplished … before that, I really didn't have anyone telling me I am a strong person … and all the things I had accomplished … so many doors would opened that I didn't know before. **I spoke my art into my existence**

For a long time, I had dreams of becoming something big. But for a while, they were only dreams. But once I said what I wanted or needed, it came alive. It came through in my art, in my painting. I matter. I learned this. Every child deserves this experience. They need it.

If anyone wanted to purchase my art, I asked for it to be donated to a women's shelter. I want women and children to feel safe. They need to feel safe and need help keeping their family together.

CHAPTER 11

SPIRITUALITY

DL

It's kinda really deep, my art, my story. I want you to understand things go on in people's lives. I want you to understand kids and everyone has a story, something to learn from. This is my justice issue. Everyone has a story. Everyone should be heard and listened to. We all need to know we can be loved. Every kid deserves that. I hope you learn from my art (see Figure 11.1).

Figure 11.1

My Art Is in a Real Exhibition

When I lived with my dad, he was a drug addict and shot up heroin in front of me. He got me hooked on meth really bad. I was 13 when I started using and that was about 2–3 years selling my body for places to stay and drugs. My dad was in and out of jail, but was I hopping around because he wasn't there (see Figure 11.2).

Figure 11.2

Someone in the Community Reading My Abstract

Nobody really wanted me. When I was younger, my uncle raped me. Pretty much, I told everyone about it. Nobody believed me. He killed himself before I told anyone. He wasn't there to defend himself, so they didn't believe me. I have talked about this so much, I don't think I can cry anymore. I feel empty sometimes … like I have no more tears to cry (see Figures 11.3 and 11.4).

When that happened to me, I was around 7, 8, or 9. It happened more than one time and he held me down. I didn't think anything was wrong with it. I was used to it. I just told my mother in therapy that my brother and I did things too. I thought it was okay to do, but I just didn't know. I was just a kid. I feel like I am the oldest, so I should have known better, but I didn't know (see Figure 11.5).

My dad didn't pretty much care…he didn't care for me at all. I was pretty much drinking all the time when I was a kid. He gave me suboxen. It's like a little pack and you open the thing, and it melts on your tongue. It's to get off hard drugs or to start them. I used to take them. My dad would leave me with them. So of course, I tried them.

Spirituality 95

Figure 11.3

Someone Using Their Phone to Read My QR Code About My Art

Figure 11.4

My Art Displayed at an Art Gallery

Figure 11.5

Someone Is Moved by My Art and What I Had to Say

My dad, I remember he made me be in the middle of shoot outs. So now, I am scared all the time. A shoot out is when two people are shooting at themselves on the street or out of the car. I was scared, so scard.

I tried to kill myself three years ago. I slit my wrist open. But my last attempt was a year ago, and I was in the ICU. I was sent to Pittsburgh hospital. I used to live there. They had called my dad and said I was ready for discharge. He said, "I don't fucking want her." Those were his words. They called my mom and told her that if she didn't come and get me, then I would be a ward of the state. She came to get me. I lived with my mom before my dad. Me and mom got into an argument, and I called my dad. He came and got me.

After my dad came and got me, my mom moved to Ohio. I didn't even know they moved … my mom, my stepdad, and my two little sisters, and a full blood brother. I was left all alone with my dad in Pennsylvania. I was on meth really bad, so I don't really remember much. I don't know. I found out through my grandma on my mom's side. I just seen her. And she told me. I started to cry.

I miss my mom. I live with her now. It's hard because I just live with her. They just send me there without us getting to know each other first. We have a lot of things on each other and we have a lot of things we went through … she calls the cops on me. So, I did seven months in a detention center for assaulting a police officer and running away. I had a warrant.

I felt unsafe at home. My mom has my uncle's pictures on the mantel and won't take them down. She said, "This is my brother. What do you want me to do? Pick sides?" I feel like things would be better if I wasn't here sometimes. I mean living. My mom tells me I am a mistake.

Things are getting better thought with us. She is being more supportive. The judge told my mom that if she doesn't do what she needs to do, she will lose me if she doesn't stop. I tell her it's not fair to ask me to look at those photos of my uncle. I don't know sometimes. My mom will wear his cologne and stuff like that. The house he did it to me in was my house and my room. I moved out of that house a while ago. It's just hard.

I am long-term here. This means I will be here for six months to a year. I really hope that me and my mom can have a better relationship. I want a healthy, non-toxic one. To be there for each other, no matter what your feelings are. She doesn't get it, but she is getting to that point. It's an adult's point of view. My counselor is on my team. If it doesn't work, then it's not safe for me to go home. I would go into independent living. There would be a bed and stuff there already. This is not even half of it. But I don't know if we will get into that today.

I realized that I am not the only one going through something. Everyone has a story. They have real things going in their lives. I read the book, "A Boy Called It" and I really relate to that book. I relate to it because a lot of things that happened to him may not have happened to me, but I felt it. It was mentally severe for me. I might as well have been through that, because that is how I feel.

As you read this and look at my art, I want you to know you are not alone. If you feel alone, I want you to read this and be touched by it. And maybe, understand it could be so much worse. That's what I felt when I read that book "The Boy Called It." Keep telling your story. Don't stop. Tell anybody you want to, but don't give your story away. Tell anybody that will listen, really listen. Maybe that person can relate to you or carry your story on and help you figure out where to go in life. They can trust God.

And God doesn't punish people. It's not God's doing. Like God doesn't punish people. Those things didn't happen to people because they are bad people. I think it's a test. It's God testing you to see how strong you are and what person you are going to be in the future (see Figure 11.6).

I don't write poetry. This is my first poem. I feel accomplished writing this. I am smiling right now, but you can't see it. I am feeling warm. I feel like I did something right in my life. I never feel like I do anything good.

People need to go through trauma,
so they know what to look out for.
I learned to love myself.
And to put myself through anything else.
I just learned that just now.
Reading and hearing my story,
I am realizing

Figure 11.6

A Closer Look

I should love myself.
I didn't feel worthy.
I am strong.
I made it.

I had watched a movie that moved me. I watched "The Shack." I loved it. God is real and everything is real, and I believe in a higher power. I watched it when I was in the detention home. I watched it by myself. I felt a connection, a real one. I felt a connection to God. It was the first time I felt a connection, that kind of connection. That was about five months ago. It makes me look at life more and telling myself don't take things for granted. It has influenced me, the movie. I shared this movie with my mom, but my mom didn't really say anything. She said it was a good movie. I didn't express my thoughts to her. I didn't tell anyone what it meant to me because ...

I usually keep my feelings to myself.
I just don't trust people.
I hope that my voice can be heard.

I am an old soul. Someone who can understand from an older perspective.

My Art

I focused on my spirit. My spirit is being optimistic and taking in different things. My face is at the center of my art because it's about me for once in my life. I was hesitant at first because nothing is ever about me. This is the first time I have ever focused on me. It feels good because I am important (see Figure 11.7).

Figure 11.7

My Art in an Art Gallery

I chose the colors because, I don't know, it touched my soul. The blues were like interesting to me. It means like my version of heaven. The white area represents the angels. They are watching over me. They are watching over me to keep me safe. I have not always been spiritual (see Figure 11.8).

Figure 11.8

Look Closer at the Darkness

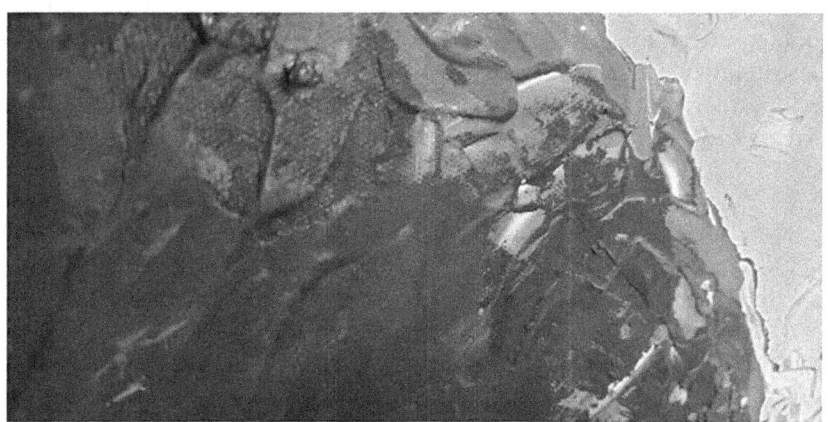

It happened when I was in detention home. I went there for assaulting a police officer. I just found myself there. It was a process. I shared that I needed God. I told myself that. Since then, I have felt lighter.

That is what I want you to see and feel when you look at my art. I want you to feel connected and spiritual (see Figure 11.9).

Figure 11.9

Look Closer at the Light

I never painted like this before. There has not been so much thought put into my art until now. I really enjoyed doing this. I did a lot of thinking. It felt good to let this out and speak my mind. I want people to care about my art and what I am saying.

It felt good to do this. I felt warm on the inside when I did this. I felt darkness before. Doing this was like feeling the light … I felt like I was talking to God. I feel my art is a part of who I am. That is a good feeling. I never felt like this before when I did any kind of art in school. It was nothing like this. It should have been like this. I don't think other kids are doing anything like this in schools.

Advice

I don't really know what advice I could give to teachers and principals. I never really thought I mattered. This is one of the first times I realize I do matter. I was actually heard. That was a first for me. I didn't have to do something a certain way. I got to express myself the way I wanted to … the way I needed.

I didn't have art like this growing up. It was just like clay. I didn't have to think about art before. It didn't have any meaning to me. This does. All kids should have the chance to do this growing up. I think they should do this with everything they learn in school. It was helpful for me, so I think it would be helpful to do this for other kids too. I think this should start when they are little kids in school and have art all the time in every school … for everything.

Teachers and principals should go to training to learn how to work with us kids and they should be educated. They need to learn how to listen to kids and let them express themselves. I would think teachers and principals would want their kids to think … and then they could learn to have the kids do this art and tell you what they learned.

If anyone buys my art, I want you to give the money to St. Judes. I learned they do so much for families that don't have. They want to make sure families have hope. My art is about hope too.

They need to care about art and kids. The bosses should watch to make sure the teachers and the principals are doing this for the kids. Art should be in every subject in school. It just made me realize things. I want that for other people. I finally felt it. That was new. We really need this in schools … bad.

CHAPTER 12

TRAUMA

T2

My justice issue is about trauma that kids go through. It's not right to put all of that on kids. I went through a lot ... didn't have anybody. Kids need to have people who love them and want them around. They need people to really care ... and that can happen at home ... and even at school ... having teachers who really care about you. I didn't have any of that.

I want to talk about my story. I made my art about my trauma. Um, you know ... me being in like the streets. Like, holding guns, stealing cars, selling drugs, doing drugs, going to jail, and then coming here. I don't know where to start. I was 15 when I held my first gun. It felt like safety. Like, I don't gotta fight with my hands. I can just pull the trigger and it would be done for me. I feel I have to fight. Like certain places or certain circumstances, you can't have a weapon to protect yourself. I felt I needed to protect myself (see Figure 12.1).

Figure 12.1

Capturing My Eye

My life was what I wanted, but my dad used to beat me. He had favoritism with my brother. He is younger. My brother would always ... my brother didn't see any wrong in my dad ... when we were broke and everything ... my brother went to live with my dad. My dad didn't like that I wanted my mom and my grandma all the time. They treated me like a princess. My dad and I didn't have a bond.

I stopped liking my dad when he broke my nose. I was like 9 or 10. My brother lied and said I bit him. He told my dad, and my dad believed him. When my dad told me to tell my brother sorry, but I wasn't going to say sorry when I didn't do it. My dad punched me in the face and broke my nose. I went to the doctor, but they couldn't do anything. My mom was scared of my dad, too. She is littler than my dad. She got beat by him too.

I remember my mom being beat by my dad. Even when I was in her stomach, my dad beat her. She was young. She got away from that. My mom drugged him to make him go to sleep. She took me and my brother with her and all of our stuff and we left. And then, and we have been by ourselves ever since. My brother doesn't like my dad no more. My dad is selfish. He only cares about himself.

I hear from my dad, but I don't really talk to him. He kinda changed because he knows I am not afraid of him anymore. He won't do anything to me. I will stab him if I need to, and he is a grown man, and I am 17 and he shouldn't be putting his hands on me ... I would show him I am not to be yelled at or hit and he don't even try to raise his voice to me anymore. He knows this too ... not to do these things. I haven't seen anybody in months. I just talk to him on the phone, but it was only for like two seconds. I don't want a relationship with him.

I have a relationship with my mom. I want to work on my communication with her and she does too, so we can actually get along with each other better. My brother is at home with my mom. I get to see him if they visit. Otherwise, he is at school. It's like sibling things. We get along and then we argue, but we're siblings. We got a good relationship, though.

My mom is safe now. She is worried about herself. She don't really do relationships anymore because my dad left her with trauma.

Trusting people is hard and loving other people. Because my dad showed me that you ... that he ... you can't trust anyone ... you should never beat your significant other ... or your child ... you should be able to trust them ... be with them without fear ... without being scared ... you should be able to tell them anything without being scared of being hit because of something you say.

I don't write poetry. These are my first two poems I ever wrote. I didn't know I was a poet. It felt nice to read them. I was smiling because it felt good to tell my story this way ...

Numb …

I am not a mean person.
I thought I could hurt someone.
I had anger inside of me.
I still do.
I used to just fight people
to get my anger out …
and do drugs …
it hurt me …
I did like being in the streets …
I could be myself f…
I could like not deal with my emotions …
my mental health …
I didn't really feel anything…
*I felt **numb**…*
that's how I coped …
I just deal with I t…
my medication helps me …
makes me feel like a zombie …
makes me focus …
and I feel more chill …
happie r…
and more calm.
That's new for me.

Trauma

I don't have a care in the world.
I am blunt.
I am loyal.
I don't trust a lot of people.
I only trust a few people close to me
but I don't really trust them either
because they can turn on me too
in the blink of an eye.
Things I trust
is my drugs and my gun.
I can count on drugs
because they make me calm
and not make me feel like a gotta be violent …
I trust my gun for my safety…
I don't gotta do nothing much to do anything to anybody …
I feel safe …
nobody wants to get shot by a gun
so they don't really mess with me.
I like the way I dress.

I just got fashion.
I got a different style.
I like my tatoos.
I got seven of them.
One is for my best friend who passed away.
The other one is for my zodiac sign.
And the other one is for my cousin
who passed away from cancer.
She passed away in 2018.
She had leukemia.
My other cousin committed suicide
two months ago.
My mom told me she had bad news.
"Your cousin committed suicide."
I didn't believe her.
I cried.
My aunt identified the body.
It was her.
My cousin hung herself.
I think because of depression.
I am triggered
when I hear about people hurting themselves
because I think of my cousin.
I don't want that around me.

People don't like me, and people want to kill me. They don't like me because my gang would beefing other gangs. I was 15. And some of my friends passed away from gun violence because of that. I wasn't there when they died. I went to the funeral. It was depressing because it was my first funeral I ever went to. He was 14. And it was traumatizing. Just seeing one of my childhood friends in a casket. It was my first funeral I ever been to, so I wasn't used to seeing someone in a casket. Um, I broke down to my knees. And I blame myself for his death. I should have been a bigger person than him. I am 17 and at the time he was 13, and I was 14, but I should have got ourselves out of that gang activity…and we should have not had that in our lives and then, he would be where he is now. I think he would be in school right now and at home with his mom. He is dead. He is in heaven. I talk to him. I talk to his pictures and stuff. I feel he is listening. I feel good but sad. Good because I can always talk to somebody, even if they are not physically here. The sad part is that I cannot hear his voice or his advice or have him physically in my space. I somewhat know it's not my fault. I don't know. I haven't processed that through. He was younger, but we should have been leaders … good leaders … instead of leading him into criminal activity … and made him a better person.

My Art

I never did anything like this before. I don't think I'm an artist … but I learned that I am. I smiled a lot and I am proud of myself. I worked really hard on this. It turned out good. Lots of people said nice things to me. I even read this to my class. I was so nervous. They were very nice to me. I even let some of my teachers read this. They really liked it. They were proud of me. I am proud of me.

I decided I wanted to use my face in my art because it's different. I got some ideas and then I wanted to do something different than I ever did before. Like I said, I never did anything like this before … I was really nervous about it … it turned out good though.

I had pictures of my face taken. This is about my story, so I used parts of my face. My art is focusing on me. I chose myself because I want people to know about me and my story. People have different stories. I want people to learn from my story. The streets is not fun and it's dangerous and it's not the lifestyle you would want. It's not safe and life is more important than being in the streets. I felt like I didn't have nobody. That's why I turned to the streets. You need to go to school and get an education. Know that there are people who care about you and love you. Yesterday, I had a hard time with the word "love." Today, I said it and it just came out of my mouth. And I am smiling again. *It tells me that i love people and people love me.*

I am smiling again. I don't know. I am happy. I wanted to make this bigger and bold because to know that people love me, and I love people.

We took a picture of my face. We cut up the photos and made it like 3-D pop out. I used a foam core to make it pop out. I painted the sides black so it would match the background. I wanted this to be like me. I want people to know I have different pieces of me and different things about me. So, each piece has words, emotions, and like about my past on them. Each part is about myself. I think each of these is important to me and who I am and my story.

I made a magnifying glass out of paper mache to go over part of my face. I used paper towel, yarn, and mod podge. The magnifying glass was used to mean that I can look at people and check them out … and they can check me out too … but just a small part. I made that part of my face, my eye, larger because that's what you would see if you were looking at me through a magnifying glass. It is on part of my face because part of it is for people to see me, but they are not looking at me all the way because I don't trust everyone. They are looking in at me and seeing a small part of who I am. As I look through the magnifying glass, I am checking them out to see if I can trust them. I am only letting them see a little part of me because I need to trust them first. I will remove this magnifying glass once I trust you.

I am wearing a white shirt because it sticks out, and it has my goals on it. Some of my goals are: (1) graduate high school; (2) go to college; (3) I want to own a business; (4) I want to own a cosmetologist business; (5) I want to be successful; (6) I want to continue to learn to trust; and (7) to love myself, love others, and to be loved by other people.

I put words in my magnifying glass to show what emotions I went through in order to check people out and make sure I can trust them: abandoned, anxiety, trauma, abuse, alone, crime, depressed, and delinquent (see Figure 12.2).

Figure 12.2

My Mouth

The hair is flowing back. It is the yarn I mod podged. Every piece of hair is next to the other. It is to show I am moving forward and not holding back. My hair is blowing in the wind (see Figure 12.3).

I used the color black for the background because it's dark, and it's me. I am dark inside. Saying the word "love" was an accident. I am smiling again. I am coming into the light. I thought I was dark on the inside. I am learning I am more than dark. I am light. I made this big and bold because I want you to know I am becoming a better person and I am about to shine ... well, a little bit now (see Figure 12.4).

The white splatters represents my white shirt I would be wearing because I want to be at peace with myself and with other people. It's the good side of me. The side that is growing (see Figures 12.5 and 12.6).

Trauma 109

Figure 12.3

My Nose

Figure 12.4

My Eyes

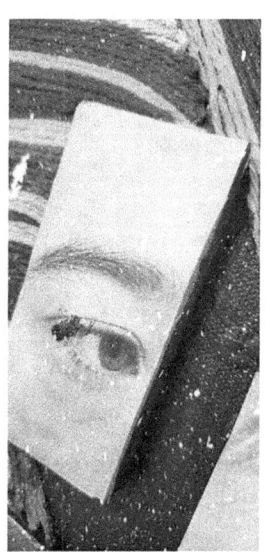

Figures 12.5 and 12.6

My Ears

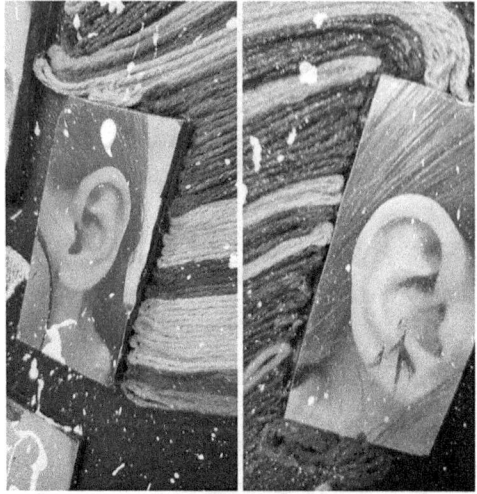

This was different for me. I am smiling now. I never did this before. It felt good to do this. It took longer to do this work. I learned to have patience. I learned to have patience with the process and with painting and doing this. When I was working on this. It was calming and peaceful. I just sang "peaceful" out loud. I am feeling relieved now that I am completing this. I am proud of myself. I did this. I never did this before. I am relieved (see Figures 12.7 and 12.8).

I think I should have art in school. People need to do art in school. They should be able to do what they like. I think art should be for all students. Everyone should be able to do this. It is just fun, and we need to have creative minds. We should be able to be creative. When I do this work, *I shine*.

Advice

I didn't go to school. I stopped going when I was in 8th grade. I was in the streets. The teachers didn't notice. They didn't notice me. I didn't have a relationship with any of them. I felt invisible. I wish they would have been there for me. They could have helped me with my problems like the stuff I was struggling with. When I was in first grade, Mr. D. supported me. He didn't judge. He would listen to me. And he was nice. I wanted to go to school because of him. It changed after first grade. No one was like him. They were not supportive (see Figure 12.9).

Trauma 111

Figure 12.7

Looking Through the Magnifying Glass

Figure 12.8

Putting It All Together

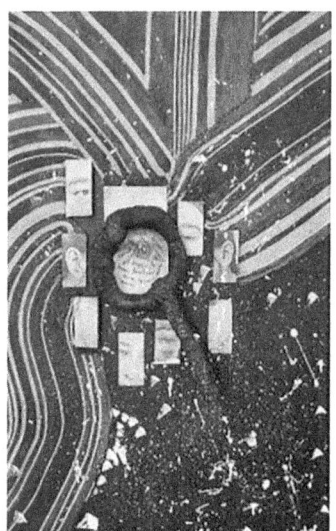

Figure 12.9

Do You See Your Students?

They was mean and rude. They didn't help. They didn't care. I felt they didn't care about me. Don't be judging kids. Be supportive. Give lots of compliments. And actually try to understand that other kids have stories, different stories. School is not just about math or reading. It's about people supporting each other and lifting each other up. You just don't know what people go through at home and school should be their safe place. They should be a teacher if they are not willing to be supportive or if they are going to be judgmental to other students. I think they should understand them. I have teachers who care about me and support me, but they don't know me. I have only been here a little bit. I don't know how long it would take. I have to let them in. That takes trust.

I am smiling again. I am trusting this. I know this isn't about being judged. I feel heard. I am listened to, and this isn't about telling my business. I am happy. I am in a good mood. I am proud of myself. I am not used to this … being proud of me. I like it. I like what I have done. I like the nice things people have said to me. I even read this to everyone in class. People said nice things. I was nervous. I did it. I am not used to talking to people in class like reading. I read this. I was nervous. I did it and I smiled. I was proud of myself. We should be doing this more in school. I never had anything like this before. I was relieved. It felt good to share my story.

Teachers and principals should be doing more of this. It should start in kindergarten. I don't know why they don't do this. I feel like they should be able to teach about this and get more into all of this. We need teachers and principals who care about us. Who loves us? If you are going to work at a job with kids, then you should love kids. You shouldn't be working there if you don't love them. Places should watch how they act when they are in classes learning to be teachers or principals. They should watch teachers and principals and how they really act when they are with kids in schools. If they don't love their kids … if they don't love kids … all kids … then they should not be allowed to work in schools. We all need love. We all need to be loved.

If someone wants to take home my art, I told them to give the money to any organization that gives kids a chance to share their thoughts … some place where they think we are important.

I didn't do anything like this before. I am in an art gallery. I am in a real art gallery. I can't believe it. People believed in me. I didn't have that before.

It's like different. I never did that before, and I don't think I would ever have a chance to do that. This is something all students everywhere should have. This was good. Real good. Everyone should have this opportunity … have this feeling inside.

CHAPTER 13

BLACK LIVES MATTER SHOULD MATTER TO EVERYONE

Moneyback King

My life matters. My justice issue is about Black Lives Matter. I want people to care about Black people. I have been through a lot since I was little. I started selling drugs when I was 10 to support my little brother and little sister. My mom really wasn't there for me when I was growing up. She was out doing drugs or with her boyfriend. She didn't care what I was doing. I basically kept leaving the house. I left every day to my friend's house and didn't come back until the lights came on and she would be looking for me. My friend gave me what he couldn't fit in, and I just stayed with him. He had his mom and his brother. They treated me like family, like I was one of their own. I don't keep in touch with them. I wish I did. He is about to be 20 and I really missed out on him and all of his birthdays. I want to hang out with him when I am older. Maybe when I am 20. I am 15 now. I don't want him to get in trouble for doing what we did. He smokes every day. He works and has a girlfriend and a dog. I want to wait to hang out with him until I am older. I appreciate his mom. I would never have been as big as I am now without her. I was so skinny. She fed me. She put structure in my life. I have not been in touch with her ... somewhat I want to be in touch with her, but for now I want to let that go (see Figure 13.1).

Personal Truths: Youth Utilizing Artmaking to Promote Diversity, Equity, Inclusion, and Belonging, pp. 115–125
Copyright © 2025 by Information Age Publishing
www.infoagepub.com
All rights of reproduction in any form reserved.

116 MONEYBACK KING

Figure 13.1

What I Think Matters

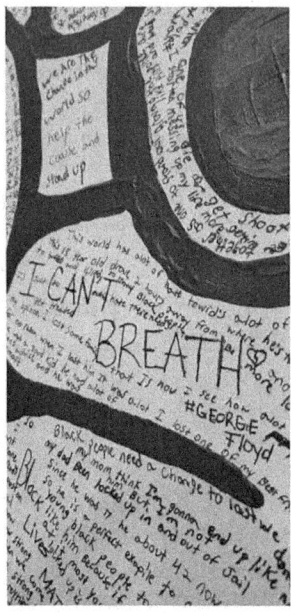

And um, I got taken away from her when I was seven. There was a drug raid in my home. The police took me away from my mom. She went to jail for a couple hours. I didn't get to go back there. I mean, I was kinda disappointed in her and our bond would be less. I was scared. That was the only person I trusted. I was so used to being with my mom. I missed my mom a lot. I lived with my grandpa and that wasn't that much of a change. My grandpa took me in … he is my father for real. He put clothes on my back and took care of me. I started stealing from him and money and took his weed … and I was realizing I was doing bad things and breaking bonds … I knew it would be a bad thing … life is too short to have this bullshit in my life … I take one day at a time, and I have to have the right mentality and I have to do that … I have to have the right mentality. My grandpa helped me. I went to school. He put me in a school right near his house. Got me clothes, shoes, food, haircuts, and gave me advice about life (see Figure 13.2).

I left my grandpa's house when I was about 13. I went to my other grandparents'. There was more structure and more discipline. I asked to go live with them. It was cool for a couple of years until I turned 14 and then I started running away more. I went to my friend's house or my mom's. I was running because of drugs. I wanted drugs to get high, and I wanted to be

Figure 13.2

My Thoughts

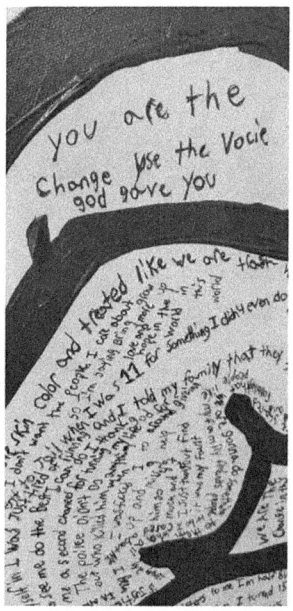

with my mom and my friends. They didn't like it one bit because they didn't know if I was safe or what I was doing. Every time I came back, they said they didn't want it to happen again. And then, my uncle would get physical with me, like a punch to my face … it was tough love. It frightened me … I was somewhat a rebel … I don't take that lightly … I got pain tolerance … I only feel it if my heads busted open … I got shot and stabbed … that was the most painful.

The most painful? So, I got shot and stabbed two years ago. I didn't buy an ex-girlfriend a pair of shoes and so she shot me and then stabbed me. She was probably 16 or 17 then. All because I didn't buy her a pair of shoes. I got paid that day. I got her a pair of Jordans on top of what I already got her and said I was cool. I was scared about what happened. She stabbed me and shot me over that. My ex-girlfriend had sex with my brother on top of that. I was sick one day. I told her come over and lay in bed with me to make sure I felt better. I got up and went to the bathroom. I caught them both, my big brother and my girlfriend having sex. I wasn't into that. I kicked their asses out … I kicked them out naked … I said "Deuces." That means "catch you later." I think she was trying to get back at me (see Figure 13.3).

118 MONEYBACK KING

Figure 13.3

People Reading My Abstract During the Exhibition

I have two older brothers … one is locked up, and the other is doing good for himself. These are my mom's adopted sons. She adopted them before she had me. I knew them my whole life. It isn't a big deal to me. My brother got locked up for grand theft auto. He is about to get out in a year. My other brother is a jeweler. He provides for everybody. He be making bank. I talk to him every day on the outs. I have not been able to talk to him. I ain't never get in trouble here. I will be out soon. I think until the beginning of June.

So, I sold drugs because I couldn't get a job when I was 10 to take care of my family and did the wrong thing. I thought she might not be there for the other two … my little sister and my little brother. I got back from prison when I was 10. My mom was a drug dealer. I took up after her. She started when I was in her stomach and has been using drugs since I was born. I got locked up on my first charge for selling drugs. I got locked up for a couple of hours. I got caught up, and I was sleeping, and I was going to drop off a bag … and I got set up by someone…and a year later, I was doing cool until my dude got out of jail … I started selling drugs again … I stopped going to school … I was 11 … I was 13 when I officially stopped going to school…and after that, there was a lot of drama. I had seen my mom getting abused since I was four…I have tried to protect her … I was her shoulder to cry on … I was her protector … I was the man of the house … when my little brother was born … I felt I needed to step up … when my little sister was born too … again, I felt like I needed to step … I just had to be there for them … to put clothes on their backs … to make sure they were learning … and to make sure they can be cool without me … I showed them how life is … it's what I learned … it's what I knew … you have to stick up for yourself … and you should be stick up for other people (see Figure 13.4).

Figure 13.4

The Public Attended the Art Exhibition

I was bullied as a kid … when I was in elementary school. I was overweight … I was a little chubby guy … oh your fat and your ugly … I wish they would say that to me now … it's cool … I would knock their teeth out … so I grew and got bigger and then they didn't pick on me anymore…

I have been in and out of jail since 10 … I was in another state … I was 13 when I got out for selling drugs and assault … I sold drugs … I assaulted a kid about my little sister … he was talking about my little sister and talking out of his mouth, so I put him in his place. His family pressed charges. I was walking out of school and picked up my little sister … he said she was ugly … she started crying and I got madder and madder and told my little sister to get in the car. And then, I took care of it. I started beating his ass. Someone had to stop me. I couldn't stop myself. I have so much anger inside of me (see Figures 13.5 and 13.6).

> So, I didn't realize this was a poem, but here it goes:
> I never had a man in my life …
> So, I fee l…
> I feel like I need to take care
> of everyone.
> It is a lot of weight on my shoulders.
> Not one single bit…

Figure 13.5

Innocent Black People Didn't Need to Die

*Not at all.
I never got to experience being a kid.
I want to be an adult.
I don't want to be no kid.
I haven't had a childhood.
So, what is having a childhood
for three years going to do?
Sometimes ...
I think ...
but I don't really trip about it.
I play basketball.
Talking.
Listening to music.
Rap ...
I rapped before I was here,
but then I stopped it.
I lost my lyrical rhythm,
but I am getting it back since I have been here.
That little boy inside of me ...
He wants to be heard.*

Black Lives Matter Should Matter to Everyone 121

He is hurting inside.
He is crying.
But,
he doesn't show it.
He is afraid to.
He is afraid of showing his emotions.
Sadness
Anger
Rage
Depression
Anxiety
Embarrassment
Just the life he has had.
That little boy is still there.
He is saying to live your life to the fullest.
Enjoy life.
Every one bit of it.

Figure 13.6

My Artmaking

When I was in jail, I got some bad news. My auntie was on the phone crying and telling me my cousin got shot … the dude was shot … his birthday is 3 days before mine … and after I got out after my first year in prison, I started using heavy drugs … smoking more … doing more pills … I knew how it would affect me … just seeing what he went through … I went to drugs … that means the road I have been struggling with until now … I dedicate this painting to my cousin (see Figure 13.7).

Figure 13.7

Example of a Person Who was Innocently Killed by Police

I am 119 days sober. I love it. I feel good. I was a runaway for two years … I was lost. I was angry. I was hurt. I did lots of drugs. But, God gave me the strength. I appreciate the teachers and everyone in this facility, honestly. I want to thank them for everything they do for me. I am trying to make my life better. I want to reach people's hearts. I love giving people advice. I love helping people out. I want to be in the NBA when I am older. I am just honestly a kid from Akron and want to be someone people can count on and give my support. It's great to be on this path right now … to show people what I can do. I want my work to be available to everyone … to inspire … I love my family…my mom, my dad, my little sister, and my little brother … my grandparents … cousins … uncles and aunts … it's just amazing being here. I bless God every day. And that's all I really got, for real. That's my life story.

My Art

My art is very powerful. I chose to focus on Black Lives Matter. This is about a movement how Black people fight back. I learned that making a fist is powerful to a lot of people. It means that we are on the same team to raise your fist (see Figure 13.8).

Figure 13.8

My Art in a Real Gallery

And basically, it is something you can like feel, know what I mean? To feel like we are a part of something. The thumb nail is red, black, and green because the colors represent the Black Lives Matter flag. I think these colors and flag help people. It helps them to see Black lives do matter and there is hope in this world. I wrote inside the fist. I wrote around and around the inside of the fist …

> Black life matters to me because us Black people get treated differently because of are skin color And treated like we are trash when we unite when one of us die or get shot we come together as one to stand our ground the police are scared that we are gonna do something to them when all we want is justice for our Black brothers and sisters to me I'm half Black so because of that Black in me people look at me different and it not fair how we get accused of something we didn't even do that is what Black life matters mean to me. I get treated differently because of my skin color for me life was hell I started selling drugs when I was 10 years old to just put food and clothes on me and my little siblings back then I went to jail when I was 11 for something I didn't even do then from that point I started messing up my life more got into drugs like pills weed and robbing people like my family friends the people who cared about me I been in and out of prison since I was 11 then when I turned 15 I realized I had to step up and stop being a kid so this last go around when I was a runaway for 2 years I turned myself in I was just tired of running and I told my family that they just want to see me do the best I can do I thank God for giving me a second chance for turning my life around.

> *Black people need a change to last we don't need hate we need peace love and support without that what do we have in life to appreciate we got ourself God and family and for what I seen it wasn't pretty my brothers and sisters stand up for me were the pride of this world my granny said I would change this world she loves the way I help everyone out my heart is the biggest one in the family.*

I also found quotes I put in the fist to show what it means to be to be Black and powerful.

"Black power is giving power to people who have not had power to determine their destiny" [Huey Newton]

"The only thing that white people have that Black people need or should want is power—and no one holds power forever" [James Baldwin]

I made the background yellow because it is a powerful color and bright like the sun. It is the hope things will change. I crossed out the faces with a red X to show these Black people were killed by the police. They are no longer here. They didn't do anything wrong, and the police killed them. These are just a few people. There were 1,021 shootings in 2021 … 1,021 in 2020 … and 38 shootings per million in 2022.

It felt pretty good to do this. I didn't think I was an artist. I learned I am. And I have a lot to say. I hope you learn from my art. I didn't think I could just do it. I did. I am proud of what I did. I did what I wanted to do. That was powerful. I was calm. I wrote a lot. I mean a lot and I learned that I want to know more about painting. I don't get to do this. I don't get to tell people what I think about too often. I did art once when I was seven. This is so much better and powerful. I felt great. I read my story to my class. It was cool. I just felt great. I thought it was very powerful.

Advice

I never learned about any of this in school. I never learned about Black life…or about Black people in a positive way. This is the first time I even talked about this with anybody, and I am about to be 16. That's wrong. I don't understand why I had to wait until now to learn this stuff.

If you want to buy my art, I want you to donate the money to any NAACP chapter. I didn't even know what the NAACP was. I just learned about it. You should too. It means the National Association for the Advancement of Colored People. They do a lot of work to protect Black people and our rights.

Everyone bleeds the same. Teachers and principals need to know this. They need to learn to respect Black people. I don't remember learning anything in school…I mean anything about Black people in a positive way. I was 9 or 10 and I learned Black people were treated differently. I didn't learn this in school. I learned this on my own.

Teachers and principals need to learn how Black people are really treated in this world. This will show them we are the same, but we are not treated the same. If they know this, then they can teach kids about the truth … the way things really are.

Art should be in schools too. It should be there for every kid. It wasn't there for me. I want to paint more now. I was heard. I actually matter. I am really interested in doing more of this.

We need to speak our hearts. We need to speak our hearts into it. I never had a chance to do this in school. We didn't even talk about anything like this. Art and learning about Black people should start when they are little. I think fifth graders could understand what I am talking about. Teachers and principals should take a test about this stuff. And if they don't pass, they don't teach. If you know your skin color, you should learn ours.

CHAPTER 14

CONSCIOUS-BASED ARTMAKING

Christa Boske

Artmaking created sacred spaces for these artists in which they engaged in courageous conversations, demonstrated care as a way of being, and committed themselves to justice-oriented work. Youth reflected on how they made meaning from their world as well as learning technical aspects of artmaking (see Greene, 1984). Artists were hesitant at first to engage in this work because they feared making mistakes. These were messages they often received from the schools they attended. As they engaged in their artmaking and sense of wonderment, they recognized this process was not skill-based; rather, it was consciousness-based. In other words, there was no rush. They embodied their art and engaged in "real time" justice-oriented work (see Greene, 1980, 1984, 1995). Youth experienced first-hand how they view life, differences, commonalities, and universal ways of being. This creative process inspired artists to discover themselves and their communities. As they engaged in their work, they deepened their sense of emotions and new ways of understanding. Their capacity to express lived experiences, knowledge, and thoughts emerges throughout this creative process.

Artists often experienced developing a strong sense of self by looking within. Throughout this process, they often experienced changes within. These changes often centered on the realization their life has purpose; the power of contributing to something larger than themselves; and the development of trusting oneself and speaking one's truth. They learned the significance of listening to oneself, acknowledging lived experiences and the influence these ways of being have on their understanding of self.

Personal Truths: Youth Utilizing Artmaking to Promote Diversity, Equity, Inclusion, and Belonging, pp. 127–130
Copyright © 2025 by Information Age Publishing
www.infoagepub.com
All rights of reproduction in any form reserved.

Artmaking afforded them spaces to determine what they deemed significant to their development of self, community, society, as well as what is not.

This person-centered inquiry created spaces to translate their understandings into developing out forms of expression, their artmaking. This process altered their ways of knowing oneself in the present, past, as well as future. Artmaking helped youth determine what matters most and their role in contributing to something larger than oneself. For some youth, these understandings stemmed from reflecting on how they came to understand the world, their beliefs, attitudes, values, and actions. They engaged in a process in which they chose to societal challenges influencing their communities, peers, school, learning, families, as well as society. Throughout this review of self, youth began to understand the power of they held by influencing the lives of others. And, artists understood how their first-tellings could encourage self-realization. In other words, as they looked within, they peeled away layers of lived experiences and ways of knowing and being to better understand one's own true self. The power of remembrance and connection emerged as a reminder of the significance of self-evolution and expansion.

Artists' works provided them with opportunities to not only recognize what mattered to them, but making meaning from their first-tellings, and expanding their capacity to contribute to their communities (see Eisner, 1994, 2002a, 2002b, 2008; Ellsworth, 2005; Springgay, 2008). Essentially, their artmaking was an unlimited, expansive experience permeating their realizations of self and others. Youth engaged in conversations about their understandings of self, their viewpoints, as how they interacted with the world. As they deepened their understanding of self, they recognized the extent their new ways of knowing and art increased their awareness of self, and for some, their spiritual path. Their work provided a sense of comfort, at times, feelings of being challenged. The process seemed to invite youth to deepen their understanding of connections with self and others. Artmaking provided a living bridge between their ways of knowing, being, and the universal spirit of humanity.

For some artists, artmaking was a release, a release of profound emotion. Their increased capacity to appreciate oneself, lived experiences, and growth contributed to their development of self. The artmaking process created a sacred space, not religious, but providing opportunities to come together, deepen understanding, engage in new ways of being, and connections among their past, present, and what is still to come. In other words, they are evolving, connected to others, and contributing to something beyond their sense of self (see Culliford, 1995). Artmaking helped them do just that.

This was the first time these artists engaged in justice-oriented work. Youth's voices were encouraged, not muzzled. Throughout their artmaking, their art captivated their values, principles, honesty, generosity, patience, perseverance, and beauty within. They recognized this artmaking process as a sacred space. Youth were valued, heard, and honored. Youth noted the role love, care, and connection made throughout this process.

These dimensions of care played a pertinent role in their capacity to embody this artmaking. They learned about stories of their peers and different people, people within their communities or elsewhere. For each person, there was a story to be told, a truth to be shared. These stories and lived experiences inspired youth to create their art, creating a sanctuary, a safe place to express oneself. As they invested in themselves, youth invested in their artmaking, which transformed their understandings into a visual story. Every work of art had a story. Nothing was created in a vacuum. We learned about the artists' intentions, their lived experiences, and what inspired youth to create this work.

Artists seemed to respond to authentic connections between the artmaking process and people working alongside them. Caring was experienced throughout this process and seems foundational to this work. Artmaking inspired youth to examine the power of self, witness the lived experiences of others, and awaken the richness each of them brings to their communities. These artists suggest schools often undermine the power of artmaking. Throughout their art, youth visually expressed their need for connection, love, authentic care, and trust. This new understanding encouraged artists to create and engage in meaningful work to foster connections between self and others. And for this art, they engaged in promoting diversity, equity, inclusion, and belonging. Their engagement promoted democratic participation by encouraging voice and decision-making, which was a shift for many of these youth (see Dewey, 1958). Their artistic expression continued to develop as they encounter validation, care, and empowerment (see Greene, 1987; Robinson, 1999). Their hope: art provides spaces for us to reflect on what inspires, enables, and moves us to new ways of thinking and being that foster authentic connections.

REFERENCES

Culliford, L. (1995). *The psychology of spirituality*. Jessica Kingsley.
Dewey, J. (1958). *Art as experience*. Capricorn Books, G. P. Putnam's Sons.
Eisner, E. (2008). Art and knowledge. In A. Cole & J. Knowles (Eds.), *Handbook of the arts in qualitative research: Perspectives, methodologies, examples, and issues* (pp. 3–12). SAGE.
Eisner, E. W. (1994). *The educational imagination: On the design and evaluation of school programs* (3rd ed.). Macmillan.
Eisner, E. W. (2002a). From episteme to phronesis to artistry in the study and improvement of teaching. *Teaching and Teacher Education, 18*(4), 375–385.

Eisner, E. W. (2002b). *The arts and the creation of mind.* New Haven, CT: Yale University Press.
Ellsworth, E. (2005). *Places of learning: Media, architecture, pedagogy.* Routledge.
Greene, M. (1980). Breaking through the ordinary: The arts and future possibility. *Journal of Education, 162*(3), 18–26.
Greene, M. (1984). The art of being present: Educating for aesthetic encounters. *The Journal of Education, 166*(2), 123–135.
Greene, M. (1987). Freedom, education, and public spaces. *CrossCurrents, 37*(4), 442–255.
Greene, M. (1995). *Releasing the imagination: Essays on education, the arts, and social change.* Jossey-Bass.
Robinson, F. (1999). *Globalizing care: Ethics, feminist theory, and international relations. Alternatives: Global, Local, Political, 22*(1) 113–133.
Springgay, S. (2008). *Body knowledge and curriculum: Pedagogies of touch in youth and visual culture.* Peter Lang.

ABOUT THE AUTHOR

Christa Boske is a Professor at Kent State University with over 35 years of experience serving schools. She is committed to social justice-oriented work in K–12 schools and underserved communities. Christa works with school leaders, teachers, students, families, and community members to promote humanity in schools.